ADVANCED PRAISE

The best leaders know the effectiveness of any leader can really only be measured by the effectiveness of the teams they build. Sadly, most leaders make up their team leadership style as they go along. Janet's book is a fantastic fast-start to any new manager who wants to become a really good leader.

~ **Paul Batz, CEO and Founder, Good Leadership**

New managers will benefit from reading and applying the learning that Janet Polach, Ph.D., brings forward in her book, *The Seven Mistakes New Managers Make: How to Avoid Them – and Thrive.* Janet embraces her years as an officer in the Marine Corps and her global consulting and coaching experience to show what these common mistakes are and demonstrates what to do instead. She also provides tools and techniques for new managers to become the leaders they wish to be. This book is timely and needed, as today new managers often lack the training necessary to develop their teams. Many were promoted to management because they were good in their individual contributor roles and are learning how to manage people as they go. An August 2020 **SHRM** survey found that 57% of American workers believe their managers could benefit from training on how to be better people managers. New managers—get this book and apply the learning to confidently manage your team and to prepare yourself for greater leadership roles going forward.

~ **Lance Hazzard, PCC, CPCC, the author of *Accelerating Leadership***

THE SEVEN MISTAKES NEW MANAGERS MAKE

Kirk House Publishers
Burnsville, Minnesota

THE SEVEN MISTAKES NEW MANAGERS MAKE

HOW TO AVOID THEM AND THRIVE

JANET POLACH, PH.D.

First Edition
ISBN: 978-1-952976-19-3
Library of Congress Control Number: 2021912515

Cover Image by: Nataliia Kokhanchuk

Published by Kirk House Publishers
1250 E 115th Street
Burnsville, MN 55337
Kirkhousepublishers.com
612-781-2815

DEDICATION

To all the managers who want to be great leaders but had no one to teach them how. Enjoy the journey of learning the right way to thrive as a manager.

ACKNOWLEDGMENTS

I learned very quickly that it takes a village to publish a book, and I had a wonderfully supportive village to accomplish the task. Two men played critical roles: My husband, Joe Polach, a retired marine lieutenant colonel and former English teacher, helped me shape my thinking and edit my flabby sentences. Rick Rittmaster holds a master's in organizational psychology and was my co-brainstormer and a critical eye in ensuring topics were covered fully and supported by previous research. Thank you both.

Others helped me make a solid book even better: Seth Johnson, Bethany Brausen, and Megan O'Connor were early readers and helped transform the manuscript from good to great. My children, Ben and Alex, provided cheerleading and great insight for millennial readers. Christine Biehl and Katie Selby, highly skilled HR professionals, and consultants Rhonda Forkrud and Terri Swenson offered additional perspective from their own experience working with new leaders.

Editor Connie Anderson from Words and Deeds, Inc. and Ann Aubitz from Kirk House Publishers topped off the team with their deep expertise for turning great ideas into something others can consume. Thank you, thank you.

TABLE OF CONTENTS

Introduction   13

Chapter 1   **Mistake 1:** Doing Instead of Leading   19
Evolve

Chapter 2   **Mistake 2:** No Plan = No Execution   27
Execute

Chapter 3   **Mistake 3:** Not Developing Your   43
Develop Your Team Team

Chapter 4   **Mistake 4:** Failure to Take Time to   57
Feedback Marketplace Give and Receive Feedback

Chapter 5   **Mistake 5:** Not Developing Your   69
Courage to Influence Power

Chapter 6   **Mistake 6:** Sticking with the Status   79
Do it Differently Quo

Chapter 7   **Mistake 7:** Not Getting Ahead of   91
Make Change Stick Change

Chapter 8   Becoming the Leader That is in You   103

About the Author   117

INTRODUCTION

Whether you are a manager of many or a team leader of a few, leading requires letting go of the day-to-day work that you had done so well as an individual contributor and instead encouraging production and achieving success through others. You most likely sought out this opportunity, maybe even dreamed about it during a college course or two—or when you were the captain of whatever sport you competed at in high school. Now the team is yours. You reached for it and were rewarded, most likely due to your hard work and success as a team member.

But how do you now ensure your success?

New managers are usually promoted because they were outstanding individual contributors: they spoke up in staff meetings, shared good ideas, and executed on time and within scope. Yet, these characteristics aren't necessarily the same ones that will make you successful as a front-line manager. Unfortunately, many organizations don't make the investment in preparing potential managers to lead, so new managers are often left on their own to figure it out. This situation is compounded because new managers feel an immense pressure to succeed. They may have been promoted above their peers and thus believe that "failure is not an option." So, they often struggle.

If this sounds familiar, then this book is for you. New managers often guess at what effective leaders do—and they often press forward through trial and error. The most common seven mistakes new managers make are outlined in this book. Each chapter highlights a common challenge that new managers face and then describes strategies and behaviors to build the skills needed to avoid these mistakes and gain success. The seven mistakes and the strategies to correct them are detailed in the first seven chapters of this book:

- **Chapter 1:** Demonstrates how to evolve from being an individual contributor to a leader of others. The mistake is staying in a *doing* mode rather than leading and working through others.
- **Chapter 2:** Describes the tools for creating an executable plan and following it through to success. The mistake is *not having a plan*, which results in not following anything and not knowing how it will be perceived by others.
- **Chapter 3:** Discusses the importance of developing your team all the time and on the job. Development is far more successful when it happens within the flow of work, so this chapter isn't about finding classes or podcasts for others to explore; it's about teaching and developing skills while individuals are completing their day-to-day work. The mistake is: simply *not taking time* to do this.
- **Chapter 4:** Identifies highly effective strategies for giving feedback to others and creating a work environment where feedback is sought out and valued by everyone. The mistake is not taking the time to give it. The tools are simple; however, sometimes, the will is a challenge.
- **Chapter 5:** Describes the challenges new managers face with taking a stand or adopting a point of view that may be unpopular but is critical to drive value. This chapter discusses how to successfully influence senior leaders and others. The mistake is not developing your power to drive tough issues forward.

- **Chapter 6:** Discusses insights and perspectives on innovation and developing opportunities to create breakthrough ideas with your team. This chapter provides numerous tools and techniques for developing breakthrough ideas with your team. The mistake new managers make is *sticking with the status quo*—and not encouraging their team to think about and discuss things differently.

- **Chapter 7:** Provides tools and techniques for managing change to help team members understand and adopt the change before it becomes a crisis. The mistake is *not getting ahead of change.*

- **Chapter 8:** Brings all the capabilities of a leader together to invite you to define the leader in you. It encourages a new leader to ask for help, to understand her or his personal style, and to take time to stay focused and recharged.

MY OWN EXPERIENCE AS A LEADER

After graduating from college with an education degree in 1980, I found it difficult to find a teaching position. However, the military advertisements caught my eye. I researched all four services, and the United States Marine Corps won—hands down. I was impressed with the Marine Corps recruiter who spoke genuinely about the corps' traditions and its guiding values of integrity, commitment, and honor. He reviewed its remarkable history that had so endeared it to Americans' hearts. I was immediately hooked, and I left for officer candidate school soon after. On a beautiful fall afternoon, I arrived in Quantico, Virginia, where I was greeted by a group of screaming seniors, enlisted marines who were charged with the task of making us officers—officers to whom they would eventually salute and report.

Throughout my academic years, I was an excellent student. However, my new experience as a marine found me wondering day-to-day, hour-to-hour, how I could possibly be successful in an organization where I knew how to do almost nothing they valued. I didn't know how to march, I didn't know how to prepare my uniform for inspection, I didn't know how to fire or clean an M-16 rifle, and I wasn't particularly athletic. However, I pushed on and persevered at learning how to do all of these things—and doing them proudly to meet the marine's high standards.

I spent the next twenty years both in active duty and the reserves, retiring as a lieutenant colonel—as one of few women senior officers, then and now. During that time, while earning my PhD at the University of Minnesota, I also worked with some of the world's premier organizations to help them become more effective and profitable.

I have spent my professional life supporting the people who do the *real* work in their organizations. Proud as I was to be a Marine Corps personnel officer, I discovered that my role was to support those on the front line in combat. Young Marine Corps officers are given tremendous responsibility: the supervision of hundreds of combat marines or the control of a $100-million aircraft. They take charge of their situations, leverage the extensive training they have received, and do what they are expected to do—accomplish their mission. These young, eager, bright professionals made a lasting impression on me. They were focused, confident, and capable. How the Marine Corps trains its young officers to become highly capable very early in their careers is phenomenal, and unfortunately, most organizations do not accomplish the same.

So, for those newly or recently promoted managers who haven't had the marine corps experience to prepare them to lead, this book is for you. Together, we will discuss the possibilities and pitfalls of leading. I leverage my years as a Marine Corps officer and my years of working with multinational corporations around the world to share with you what works and doesn't work in order to help you avoid the pitfalls and mistakes new managers often make.

Good luck on your journey!

Janet Polach, Ph.D.

I can be reached at *janet@inthelead.co*
www.inthelead.co
612.500.7069

Chapter 1

EVOLVE

Mistake 1: Doing Instead of Leading

I was first introduced to the V-22 Osprey as a marine second lieutenant in the 1980s. The Osprey is a joint-service combat aircraft utilizing tiltrotor technology to combine the vertical performance of a helicopter with the speed and range of a fixed-wing aircraft.

While the V-22 first flew in 1989, its complexity and the difficulties
of being the first tiltrotor aircraft led to years of development, disappoint-
ments, fatalities, and cost overruns prior to its official introduction to the
Marine Corps in 2000. After descending vertically to drop off or collect
ground-combat troops, the Osprey tilts its rotors to the horizontal position to move at speeds up to 270 knots, nearly twice the speed of a traditional helicopter—a high-need capability but one that had escaped the military for years. Yet, the value of this amazing aircraft is also its greatest
risk. As the aircraft gains speed, the rotors are progressively tilted forward,
becoming vertical. In their vertical position, the rotors provide thrust to
propel the forward motion of the entire aircraft, allowing combat-ready
marines to descend quickly into enemy territory, inserting troops or

retrieving casualties and then exiting the area in flight at speeds previously unimagined.[1] Since being operationalized throughout the corps in 2007, the V-22 Osprey has been deployed in transportation and medevac operations over Iraq, Afghanistan, Libya, and Kuwait and has been used for worldwide disaster relief. Plans are underway to deploy the Osprey for carrier operations in 2021.[2]

This amazing capability of changing from vertical lift to horizontal propulsion while in flight is comparable to the transition from being an individual contributor to manager in many organizations.

Individual contributors:

- Understand goals and priorities;
- Use time and resources effectively to solve assigned tasks;
- Solve problems related to their work;
- Deliver results; and
- Expand their contribution by learning and growing professionally.

Managers, on the other hand, *work through others*. They:

- Set expectations for others;
- Manage team relationships;
- Deploy resources;
- Make decisions;
- Communicate progress and issues;
- Deliver on time; and
- Develop others.

If the responsibilities of an individual contributor were compared with typical manager capabilities, one would quickly observe that some, but certainly not most, of the responsibilities and the skills needed to accomplish them are quite different. Yet, organizations across the world promote individuals into manager roles because they are successful individual contributors.

Individual Contributors
- Understand responsibilities
- Execute tasks
- Report progress
- Learn and grow

Managers
- Plan
- Execute
- Communicate
- Develop others

During the transition from individual contributor to manager, some but not all skills and capabilities are discarded, while others are required and must be developed.

The work of the manager differs from the work of the individual contributor in significant ways. Managers have:

- Larger scope and more complex responsibilities;
- Broader decision-making responsibilities;
- Impact on the organization at a higher level than do individual contributors; and
- Responsibility for transforming the organization's strategies and delivering on the quarter's plan.[3]

Fundamentally, executing on the quarter's plan incorporates these four overlapping dimensions:

- **Planning** – Managers plan the work of others and define the path for achieving success. They are responsible for not only their own success but the success of their team, regardless of whether the team is two individuals or a plant of two thousand employees. They set reliable and challenging targets; they estimate levels of effort needed, given the composition of the staff; and they set timelines for achieving each goal.
- **Executing** – Managers achieve success and build their reputation by delivering on the plan. Detailed plans created with the team are easier to deliver when the entire team knows what is

expected, in what timeline, and within what quality specifications. Managers early in their tenure may make assumptions about responsibilities because they once contributed as individual contributors. However, it's necessary to quickly gain clarity on what's expected and which year-to-date goals are being achieved, as well as where a team might be coming up short.

- **Communicating** – Managers share information with their teams proactively. They must possess a keen sense of which communication vehicles are most effective and be aware of whether information can be shared now or must wait for a later time. Managers use communication to connect their teams to each other and to the broader goals of the organization.
- **Developing others** – Finally, and perhaps most importantly, managers must take time to enhance the capabilities of their team. They provide feedback, encouragement, and resources for broadening the skill mix needed now and in the future across the team. They encourage professional development and create opportunities for learning, both formally and informally.

The Transition Challenge

Employees frequently view promotions to a managerial position as a positive career experience. However, many new managers find this transition to be more challenging than they had expected. Individuals in professional, scientific, or technical positions develop a professional identity that is highly associated with their expertise and educational background. Individuals are often promoted to manager positions because of their high level of technical skills and performance. Work and the value placed on outstanding performance are often key to professional and personal identity. Transitioning to a new and unfamiliar role of a manager, regardless of how ready we believe we are, can be challenging emotionally. In addition, new managers need to make a shift in how they measure their personal success and how they derive personal satisfaction.[3]

Managers are measured by their success through others. Moving from individual contributor to manager is a journey. While there is excitement in the promotion, Park and Faerman, authors of *Becoming a Manager: Learning the Importance of Emotional and Social Competence in Managerial Transitions,* discovered that the initial transition is characterized by feeling overwhelmed, anxious, and sometimes frustrated.[4] Fundamentally, becoming a successful manager is about *reframing.*

Ask yourself:

- How do I achieve success without doing the work?
- How do I engage others to complete the work when they may not be as motivated as I am?
- How do I tap into other's creativity and great ideas when others don't proactively share their insights?

Developing a mindset of working through others is a critical first step. The transition is made even more difficult for many because managers are often promoted from within their peer group. Meet Nia, an HR manager at a mid-sized public-school district in the suburbs. She was promoted to manager from within her team two years ago. "I learned very quickly that I had to set boundaries. I couldn't be a friend anymore, or at least I had to be a friend in a different way." Nia quickly discovered that there were a few performance issues on the team that had lingered, issues she wasn't aware of as a team member. "These people had been my friends, so it was awkward at first." Additionally, she realized that she was much younger than some of the team members she now managed, which added to the awkwardness. But she acted on issues and others seemed grateful. Performance issues had lingered with the previous manager. Nia built her credibility over time, but it was difficult. She gained confidence through trial and error—but wished her organization had prepared her for the transition.

Prepare for the Transition Ahead of Time

Becoming a manager for the first time can be a satisfying learning experience. The key is preparation before it happens. Consider the strategies below for preparing for the transition.

- **Clarify why you want to be a manager.** Being an effective manager is more than just a salary increase. Great managers fundamentally enjoy engaging and encouraging others. Take time to define why being part of management makes sense.
    - Ask yourself . . . do I:
    - Like to be in the know?
    - Like to build and develop others?
    - Want more information firsthand?
    - Want to be responsible for accomplishing broader goals?
    - Begin to articulate your goals for being a manager before you're given the opportunity so that you're clear on your motives.
- **Study great managers.** There are great managers and lousy managers. We can learn from both. Identify two or three great managers you work with and observe what makes them special. Interview them and discover their professional journey. Find a podcast or TED Talk that explores great leadership, and then identify the behaviors you want to incorporate into your own persona.
- **Separate yourself from your colleagues.** If a promotion is at hand, prepare yourself by separating yourself from your colleagues. Having lunch together is fine but probably not happy hours, at least until your manager role and your new relationships with your team have been firmed up. Identify what you want others to say about your leadership abilities—and then identify how to incorporate those behaviors in your leadership routines.

- **Clarify expectations immediately.** Upon being promoted, set clear expectations with your manager. What does your boss expect: turn around, status quo, new capabilities? Be deliberate during your initial weeks as a new manager. Craft plans to achieve success. Meet with each team member to clarify expectations, and then communicate regularly on progress across the team.

Perhaps, most importantly, lead with grace, primarily for yourself but also for your team. You won't get it right the first time. In fact, you'll get a number of things wrong. You won't be perfect; no new leader ever was. So read this book with that in mind.

Like the tiltrotor of the V-22 Osprey, thinking like the boss is a different experience than thinking like an individual contributor. The transition can be difficult, but many have been successful. It comes with time, but it also comes with effort. Get clear on your goals for becoming a manager, and then seek feedback often on how you are doing once you're there.

References

1. See reference to the U.S. Marine Corps Osprey in full deployment status. https://web.archive.org/web/20161201231225/http:/www.navair.navy.mil/v22/index.cfm?fuseaction=news.detail&id=178; *https://www.boeing.com/defense/v-22-osprey/*

2. Kreisher, Otto. *Finally the Osprey.* https://www.airforcemag.com/article/0209osprey/

3. Eichinger, Bob, & Pearlman, Roger. (2018). *DIY: Develop It Yourself: The Development Guide for Managers or Supervisors.* TeamTelligent.

4. Park, Hyun Hee & Faerman, Sue. (2019). *Becoming a Manager: Learning the Importance of Emotional and Social Competence in Managerial Transitions,* American Review of Public Administration, Vol. 49 (1) 98-115.

Chapter 2

EXECUTE

Mistake 2: No Plan = No Execution

General Dwight D. Eisenhower, the thirty-fourth President of the United States, rose to influence while serving as supreme commander of the Allied Expeditionary Force in Europe during World War II. He was responsible for the planning and invasion of Operation Torch in North Africa and the successful invasion of Normandy, France, by allied forces in 1944, which ultimately led to the end of the war. A calm and capable leader, he rose to prominence through hard work and a humble demeanor and is profiled in David Brooks's book, *The Road to Character*, which considers the deeper values that inform our lives.[1] Eisenhower served as president from 1953 until 1961. He is noted for stating, "I have found in battle that plans are useless, but planning is indispensable." The key to successful execution is the act of planning, of engaging others in setting targets, enumerating options, considering challenges, and then agreeing on a course of action. In dozens of speeches during his army career and presidency, Eisenhower regularly harkened back to this insight when discussing the value of engaging others and considering options prior to agreeing on a course of action. This discussion, this planning, he argued, is key to delivering successfully when the execution of plans, as they always do, go astray.

Even for new managers, one key success is the ability to effectively adopt the basic elements of planning and execution. Managers must understand what is expected of them and their team, encapsulate that into a plan with the help and collaboration of their team, and then communicate the plan to the team, their leader, and other stakeholders. Planning and eventual execution involve translating the enterprise strategy into a workable, tactical way forward. Managers must decide the path to follow when given myriad options. They must identify the tasks needed to execute the plan and by whom they will be performed, how progress will be measured, and what contingencies should be considered when issues arise. Planning and execution are critically important to a manager's reputation and ultimate success, yet too often, new managers assume that results will just happen, particularly when they take leadership over from an existing team that is already performing.

Managers who plan and execute well:

- Articulate the link between the organizational mission and the team's plans;
- Engage their team in setting goals and developing strategies for accomplishing goals;
- Identify the team's top priorities—and apply resources to those first;
- Deliver projects and results on time and within budgets;
- Establish progress measures and monitor progress;

- Leverage people resources fully and garner additional resources for short-term solutions to delivery challenges;
- Identify milestones and work with their team on progress as well as the barriers to success; and
- Communicate progress to the team, the boss, and other stakeholders.

Successful planning and execution involve several components. A useful resource that provides insight and guidance for creating high-performing teams in any organization is Doug Smith and Jon Katzenbach's book, *Wisdom of Teams*[2]. The authors interviewed hundreds of work groups and teams. They concluded that not all teams are the same, and they vary based on the firm's purpose for the team. They identified key components to nearly every team's success, whether large or small. Over the years, I've used this model countless times with teams and have modified it as needed. Highly successful managers use the components below to drive their team's success.

Team Framework

Start with Purpose	Purpose describes why the team exists and articulates why it takes a team to make it happen.
Create Team Goals	Team goals transform the organization's higher purpose into relevance for the team. They define how the team will accomplish their assigned goals and expectations.
Align Goals to Team Members	Individual goals segment the collective skills of the team and assign work based on each individual's skills and motivation. Check on progress regularly throughout the year.
Mutually Deliver Results	Results, coupled with verifiable measures in terms of cost, quality, and quantity, are the concrete way a team demonstrates its success.
Build Trust and Sustainability	Trust is at the heart of every interaction and every functioning team. It is the how the work gets done.

It Starts with Purpose

New or inexperienced managers often fail to set a strategic vision. They often don't conceptualize what their department will become in three to five years or how they might take on significantly different responsibilities. They need to articulate a purpose for the team, which is the center post for all team activities.

Accomplishing goals and delivering results begins fundamentally with knowing why the team is a team. New managers may take this step for granted because they assume that everyone on a team knows the purpose. But it's a critical step. The team purpose describes why the team exists and articulates why it takes others to accomplish the work itself.

As leaders, we often assume that the team knows its purpose. The purpose explains what the team is expected to achieve and what value the team brings to the organization. Team purpose is different than a company vision because it is specific and defining to the team itself. It can include what the team does and sometimes what the team doesn't do.

Here are a couple examples:

- We are the ABC team, formed to provide immediate technical support with single interaction resolutions wherever possible for all XYZ employees.
- Our team is committed to the maintenance, repair, and cleanliness of our 105-year-old church in order to ensure a comfortable, safe, and quality experience for our congregants, worshippers, visitors, and staff.
- The team purpose is best created by the team itself. Although unique to the team, it rests inside the organization as a whole. A complete and compelling team purpose includes:
- The team's outcome: what is it expected to accomplish, by when, and for what purpose
- Aligning or enabling the goals of the broader organization
- Expressing it in a way that is understood by all team members

The U.S. Marine Corps employs a tactical tool across all ranks, referred to as the five-paragraph order. This tool specifies the instruction to a unit in a format that makes it easy to understand what is expected in terms of an immediate mission. Like all things military, the five-paragraph order comprises an acronym, in this case: Situation, Mission, Execution, Administration/Logistics, and Command/Signal (SMEAC). This standard format is taught to privates and lieutenants alike. A singular but important point included in the mission is the commander's intent. The commander's intent describes the broader scope of the mission. The commander signals his intent by the words, "in order to." These simple but profound three words bring great clarity and provide a broader context for the mission. An example: "In order to safely secure the perimeter for the landing force, we will . . ." This explanation informs unit leaders—and if incapacitated, these unit leaders are next in line—how to achieve the assigned mission while supporting the broader outcome. To think like a boss in your organization, ensure that all team members know and understand the team's purpose statement so that they are empowered to make decisions during their daily and weekly tasks.

Goals Follow Purpose

Team performance goals vary from year to year. While we would like to think that performance goals are set by the team, they are often assigned to the team by higher leadership. However, the team can take the higher directives and make them their own, discussing *how* they will accomplish their assigned goals and expectations. Taking time to do this creates clarity for each team member so they, in turn, can identify their own individual goals to support the team's goals.

The author of *The Five Dysfunctions of a Team: A Leadership Fable*, Patrick Lencioni,[3] has written extensively about the performance of teams. He urges leaders to take time discussing and understanding performance goals because they create buy-in and clarity for understanding what each goal really means. They could include the following:

- Quality: what is the standard for completing the work? Quality measures include accuracy, speed, or ability to repeat a result.
- Reporting: how progress will be monitored and reported. Is it hourly, daily, weekly? What is the input required for effective monitoring and reporting?
- Milestones: How will interim steps be captured and celebrated? How will adjustments be made if progress is lagging?

Engaging at a deeper level in discussions on team performance goals fosters team development. The specificity of performance objectives facilitates clear communication and constructive conflict. The attainability of specific goals helps teams maintain their focus on achieving results.

Set Individual Goals

Teamwork divides the work and multiplies the success. However, this only happens if everyone on the team knows how they fit into that purpose. Let's face it, not everyone is great at everything—even our most talented resources. A wise manager considers the collective skills of the team and then assigns work based on both skills and motivation.

Start by considering each employee's personal career aspirations. What do they aspire to become? What are their hopes and dreams? How can they further their aspirations in the work they are doing today? A timeworn tool that helps managers more deeply assess goals for individuals is the Skill/Will Matrix. First introduced by Max Lundberg in his book, *The Tao of Coaching*[4], originally published in 1966, the Skill/Will Matrix helps a manager think about not only capability but also motivation for each employee.

- **Will** is on the horizontal axis. Is the person motivated or engaged to do the work? Is the work interesting and engaging for them?

- **Skill** is on the vertical axis. Does the person have the necessary capabilities or know-how to get the job done? Do they need to acquire additional knowledge or skills in order to accomplish the task?

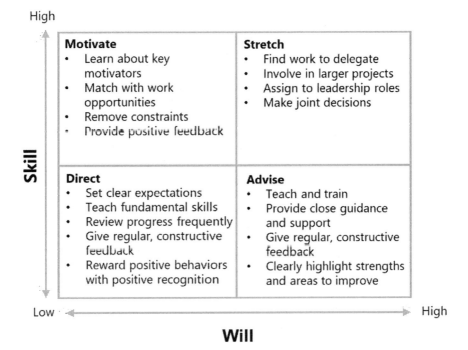

High

Motivate
- Learn about key motivators
- Match with work opportunities
- Remove constraints
- Provide positive feedback

Stretch
- Find work to delegate
- Involve in larger projects
- Assign to leadership roles
- Make joint decisions

Direct
- Set clear expectations
- Teach fundamental skills
- Review progress frequently
- Give regular, constructive feedback
- Reward positive behaviors with positive recognition

Advise
- Teach and train
- Provide close guidance and support
- Give regular, constructive feedback
- Clearly highlight strengths and areas to improve

Skill

Low ← → High

Will

Depending on the answer to these questions, the person will fall into one or more quadrants on the grid based on individual tasks or goals that need to be accomplished. Coaching and development of each individual can be revealed in the placement. Below are strategies for addressing individuals in each quadrant:

- **Low Skill/Low Will:** This individual may not be worth the effort. Set clear expectations for a given timeline and then see what happens. Make certain they are properly trained for the work they are expected to deliver. Check in regularly to discuss progress and give feedback—both recognition and constructive.

- **High Skill/Low Will:** Find out what's going on. Is the person bored? Struggling with a newly assigned task and won't ask for help? Take time to share your observations. This individual may not be aware of their motivation has changed. Reestablish expectations and find out what will re-engage them. Would they like to teach others? Take on a different role?
- **High Will/Low Skill:** Find more of these individuals! They are eager and willing to learn. Identify what interests them and ascertain their learning style. Consider pairing them with a High Skill/Low Will individual to learn and grow. As they learn, highlight their successes and provide corrective feedback, if necessary, so they won't develop bad habits or incorrectly learn a new skill.
- **High Skill/High Will:** Delegate, but don't dump. Identify things they do well and share the workload with them. Challenge them with new learning or skills, but interact with them regularly so that they don't feel forgotten.

Complete a Skill/Will assessment on your staff every six months. Ascertain engagement, possibilities for learning new skills, and opportunities for employees to teach others.

Regularly Check on Progress

Holding a regular one-on-one (1:1) with each employee is one of the practices found in Franklin Covey's *Six Critical Practices for Leading a Team* development program. A recurring weekly or biweekly thirty-minute meeting allows you to check in with employees on a regular basis to learn what they are working on, identify barriers or challenges for completing the work, and determine how they are connecting to their work in general. Over time, encourage your employee to take the lead on these meetings after you've established a routine.

- **Start by discussing achievements.** What has been accomplished since the last time you met? Take time to understand not only what was accomplished but how it was accomplished. What was learned? What new skills or abilities are being learned from this responsibility? What could be done differently next time?

- **Discuss upcoming work.** Find out what's on the horizon and whether the employee has any concerns about accomplishing what's expected. This is a great time to be forewarned if projects or tasks may not be on track—before they reach a crisis point. Avoid offering suggestions or advice for how *you* would do it. Listen, listen, listen, and ask questions for clarification. Identify any actions you might take to support their efforts—but only if requested.

- **Summarize what was covered.** Build the habit of having the employee summarize the meeting to ensure you both heard the meeting the same way. Assign deadlines to action items and take notes to make sure you don't overlook your own responsibilities. Thank each employee for their time, and show appreciation for the work they are doing.

Drive Mutual Accountability for Results

The true measure of a great team is that it *accomplishes the results it sets out to achieve.* Integrating each team members' capabilities and working in a productive, engaging way is critically important to accomplishing the intended results. With clear goals articulated, teams can avoid distractions because team members are prioritizing the results. In delivering results, the work of the team is a true reflection of the manager's capabilities. Are they going to hit targets? Exceed them? Results on a team are delivered through mutual accountability. After all, if the team does not share accountability for the work of the team, it isn't really a team—it's just a group of people all working on the same things.

Fundamentally, managers complete their work through others. Effective leaders track and aggressively communicate progress so that everyone stays on the same page about what is expected—and whether progress is being made. Whether you're an Excel wizard or not, create simple visuals to help team members understand goal progress and to identify challenges that they may be facing. Keep progress visible by posting it publicly or including it regularly in team updates. Remember to orient new team members on the team's purpose, goals, and communication tools.

Finally, take time to evaluate progress as a team. Set aside time regularly (every other month, for example) to evaluate what's working for the team and how the team might be struggling in accomplishing their goals. Create opportunities for input from all team members and offer suggestions for moving forward rather than laying blame.

Team members know that some decision is better than no decision and that it is better to make a choice, act with boldness, be wrong, and change direction than it is to waffle or wait for 100 percent certainty. High-functioning teams unite behind a decision even though there is no certainty that the decision is correct. Teams with a strong level of accountability understand that members do not need to get their way to support a decision but only need to know that their opinions have been heard and seriously considered. Commitment requires clarity and buy-in. Clarity requires that teams avoid assumptions and ambiguity and that they end discussions with a clear understanding of decisions that they have made. Buy-in does not require consensus. Members of great teams learn to disagree with one another and still commit to a decision.

Build Trust and Sustainability

How the team works together is as critical as what the team delivers. Ineffective interactions can cause stress and even hostility, but working relationships also impact productivity, the ability to get things done, and the quality that the team produces.

Hundreds of books have been written about great teamwork, and there are hundreds of analogies around team effectiveness. Think of a champion sports team or a world-class orchestra. Both create excellence by *how* they do their work. High-functioning teams work well together while producing quality results.

Of course, it starts with trust. Trust is built and maintained over time by actions, or inactions, from the leader or other team members. Trust is at the heart of every interaction and every functioning team.

Trust can develop over time by utilizing a few time-tested strategies:

- **Team members establish and follow team norms.** Effective teams take time to establish working guidelines and check in on guidelines from time to time to make sure they are being followed and are useful in getting the work done.

- **Team members provide regular and ongoing feedback to each other.** Team members are comfortable giving feedback to others outside of the regular performance-management system. They feel comfortable giving ad hoc recognition and suggestions to ensure expectations are in sync with one another.

- **Teams orient new team members.** This is often overlooked. Trust needs to be rebuilt when new members are added to the team. They need to be oriented on team expectations, norms, and practices. If not, they may cause disruption in "the way things are done here" and not even know it.

- **Conflict is part of the team's workings.** High-functioning teams know that conflict is a critical part of effective teamwork. All teams naturally have conflict. When people work together and they are committed to what they are doing, disagreements in perspectives or how things should be done will arise.

- **The team has fun together.** Finally, effective teams build fun into their day-to-day work. They celebrate successes and find ways to create joy. These informal interactions create psychological safety for team members. They feel more included and will most likely give more to the team.

When to Give Up and Let Go

Sometimes, regardless of all your hard work, an employee just doesn't work out. You've trained, encouraged, and given feedback, but the performance is still substandard. What then? First, remember, it's not you. Not everyone is able to perform well in every position, regardless of how well they performed during an interview. Some people are in a place in their lives where they can't achieve, regardless of the support given. So, what then?

First, don't wait too long—thirty days is plenty of time to see progress. If you don't see it, work with your HR partner to begin a progressive discipline plan; most organizations have them. Document the minimal expectations and outline where the employee is falling short. Articulate actions that must be taken to return the performance to satisfactory. Check in with them frequently and note things that are going well and not so well. After thirty days, make a decision.

Termination decisions are difficult because they involve someone else's livelihood. However, they can be done with dignity and grace. Remind the person why they are being terminated and exit them from the organization. Again, utilize your human resource professional to guide you in what you can and cannot say to an individual.

One final note: don't wait too long. It's usually clear to see whether someone will be successful or not. Waiting more than thirty days for improvements only prolongs the pain and discomfort for you, the employee, and most likely the rest of your team.

Assess Your Team's Health

Wondering about the health of your team? Consider using this simple assessment to garner perspective from team members and to foster productive discussions on team health. Ask team members to complete their own assessment and then collectively discuss the results. Be surprised and delighted by what you uncover!

	Strongly Disagree	Disagree	Neither	Agree	Strongly Agree
Team members collaborate developing team vision/purpose.					
My performance goals are aligned to the overall team vision/purpose.					
The work of the team is evenly distributed across all team members.					
Team members provide regular feedback to one another.					
Conflict is recognized and managed in a healthy manner.					
The team has clearly established goals.					
Team members express confidence in the group's ability to meet goals.					
The collective skills of the team make the team successful.					
Team members look for solutions rather than blaming others.					
Team members show respect for one another.					

Teams are at the heart of the manager's job. Whether a team is as small as three people or as many as dozens, the manager's fundamental job is to deliver expected results for the team by leading, guiding, and directing team members toward success. This happens when managers engage their teams throughout the purpose and goal-setting process and hold regular performance check-in meetings with each employee. They ensure that each employee is recognized for the work they are doing well and that they are delivering on time and within quality standards. Effective managers encourage teamwork and create an environment where feedback is freely given and freely accepted. They recognize hard work and reward the team for work well done.

References

1. Brooks, David (2015). *The Road to Character.* New York, NY: Random House.
2. Katzenbach, Jon and Smith, Douglas K., and Katzenbach, Jon (2015). *The Wisdom of Teams: Creating the High-Performance Organization.* Cambridge, MA: Harvard Business Review Press.
3. Lencioni, Patrick (2002). *The Five Dysfunctions of a Team: A Leadership Fable.* San Francisco, CA: Jossey-Bass.
4. Lundberg, Max (2015). *The Tao of Coaching.* London, England: Profile Books

Chapter 3

DEVELOP YOUR TEAM

Mistake 3: Not Developing Your Team

"But I'm not a teacher!" is a common reaction from a new manager when he's been encouraged to develop his team. The good news: you don't have to be a professional educator to facilitate learning on and within your team. So, the first barrier for new managers to overcome is moving from "that's not my job" to "this *is* my job."

Effective leaders build learning into the daily and monthly work of the team. Some set aside time for deliberate learning by encouraging team members to attend courses or explore special interests on company time. Others take time to check in on learning during team meetings or during 1:1s.

Ask yourself:

- What did I discover about myself?
- What is difficult about the new skill I am acquiring?
- What have I found myself doing differently?

Managers Who Work Hard to Develop Others

One of the best bosses and leaders I ever had a chance to work for was Lieutenant Colonel Dave Nelson. He was the squadron commander of an advance maintenance helicopter squadron at New River, North Carolina, where I was stationed as a second lieutenant. Shortly after he arrived at the command, he and I spent several weeks "aligning the Table of Organization" or T/O. Every unit across the Marine Corps has a T/O, and it specifies how many marines and which occupational specialties each unit should have on board. This allowed for, among other things, marines to be properly trained and ready for any mission they were asked to perform.

When he arrived, our squadron was a mess. We had marines who weren't fully trained to perform advanced maintenance functions, and in other cases, we had too many highly skilled marines in certain specialties, potentially shortchanging adjacent squadrons of their highly trained and badly needed expertise. One day, as we worked through this task, he asked, "Jan, do you even know what these people do?" As a human resources officer, I knew how to promote people and adjudicate their orders to other duty stations, but I had no idea what a HeloAFMech actually did. Understanding the task was made more difficult because on my computer printout, all specialties were listed in cryptic descriptions such as this, along with a four-digit numeric indicator called a military occupational specialty, or MOS. He paused and explained to me what a helicopter airframe mechanic actually did and how they were specialized by aircraft. And then he asked, "I bet you don't know what half of these jobs are about, do you?"

"No," I confessed. He picked up the phone and called Top Spencer. Master Gunnery Sergeant Spencer was the maintenance chief for the entire squadron. He asked him to give me a tour of the maintenance shop. Top Spencer loved his job and his marines; he was delighted to spend well over two hours with me pointing out what various marines did, which ones were highly skilled, and how they worked together. This grand tour made my job much easier.

This event was a classic on-the-job training experience because it occurred naturally. There wasn't an aircraft maintenance overview course I could have taken, even if I had wanted to, but I learned an important aspect of my job during that short tour. The most meaningful kind of learning is found in the flow of the work. When Lieutenant Colonel Nelson saw an opportunity for learning, he seized the moment. He took the time to develop a young marine officer so she would be more capable and more respected in her role.

Managers who do a good job of developing others:

- Take time during team meetings to capture from others what has been learned;
- Encourage team members to take time for formal and informal learning;
- Share what they know and encourage others to do the same;
- Deliberately establish cross-team mentoring relationships to broaden the collective skills of the team;
- Evolve a team that previously struggled to deliver results; and
- Become known informally as a developer and promoter of talent.

While learning in the flow of the work has the most impact, leaders can encourage their teams to engage in learning in other ways: through others, from reading, or from traditional online or in-person courses. Regardless of format, learning within the job and adding skills to what individuals already know enhances their organizational commitment and, ultimately, improves rates of retention.

Know What Areas You Need to Develop

In the Planning and Execution chapter, I encouraged you to establish team goals that define what the team will be expected to accomplish and then identify individual goals for each team member based on their skill and motivation.

I suggested to start by considering each employee's personal career aspirations. What do they aspire to become? What are their hopes and dreams? How can they further their aspirations in the work they are doing today? We reviewed the Skill/Will Matrix. Skill/Will helps a manager think about not only capability but also motivation for each employee.

- **Will** is on the horizontal axis. Is the person motivated or engaged to do the work? Is the work interesting and engaging for them?
- **Skill** is on the vertical axis. Does the person have the necessary capabilities or know-how to get the job done? Do they need to acquire additional knowledge or skills in order to accomplish the task?

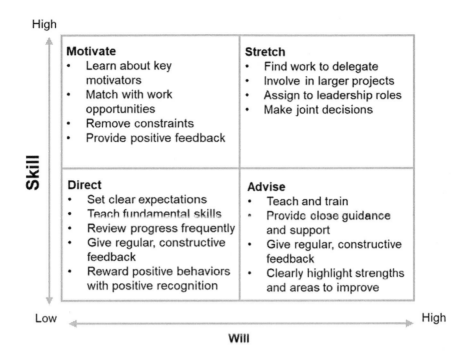

High

Motivate
- Learn about key motivators
- Match with work opportunities
- Remove constraints
- Provide positive feedback

Stretch
- Find work to delegate
- Involve in larger projects
- Assign to leadership roles
- Make joint decisions

Direct
- Set clear expectations
- Teach fundamental skills
- Review progress frequently
- Give regular, constructive feedback
- Reward positive behaviors with positive recognition

Advise
- Teach and train
- Provide close guidance and support
- Give regular, constructive feedback
- Clearly highlight strengths and areas to improve

Skill

Low — Will — High

Goals, whether team goals or individual goals, are the *what* of performance; the skills or competencies are *how* the work gets accomplished. To perform well, employees need to know what is expected of them and have the skills to perform the tasks required. A competency model is a framework for defining the skill and knowledge requirements of that job. This tool defines successful job performance. Competency models are widely used in business for defining and assessing capabilities within organizations in both technical and interpersonal skills. And they can identify where additional skill-building is needed.

Whether imparting technical skills such as completing a month-end financial closure or running software testing or imparting interpersonal skills such as collaborating or solving problems, effective leaders find opportunities for their team to develop skills on the job and, of course, through traditional formal-learning programs. Setting the expectation that learning happens throughout the course of the workday is key.

Not All Learning Opportunities Are Created Equal

Many learning professionals use the 70/20/10 model to outline learning in the context of the workplace. The model was created in the 1980s by three researchers at the Center for Creative Leadership: Morgan McCall, Michael Lombardo, and Robert Eichinger. It's a learning and development framework that suggests a proportional breakdown of how people learn most effectively. It offers organizations a way to think about employee development, concluding that not all development should occur in a classroom setting.[1]

70%: On-the-Job or Hands-on Experiential Learning.

These are aha moments and insights gained during the application of concepts learned through informal learning within the job setting. This method allows team members to learn new skills, often from each other, within the flow of the work. The model's creators argued that hands-on learning experiences are most beneficial for employees because they enable them to learn within the framework and constraints of their job. It involves trial and error while performing the job and requires feedback to be provided when new skills are tried. Keep in mind that you can leverage formal learning on the job. For example, create a weekly learning activity with your team by watching a favorite TED Talk or podcast. Listen together and then discuss. This is a great way to demonstrate to your team that learning matters and that it's part of their day-to-day work life.

20%: Networking, Mentoring, and Coaching.

Learning is deepened, reinforced, and aligned when people are encouraged to discuss and debrief with peers and mentors what they are learning or attempting to do differently in a highly collaborative way. This method, learning from others through networking or mentoring, is often the most under-utilized approach to learning I have found. Encourage your team to expand their networks and find mentors who are not direct supervisors but are within their work environment who can mentor them about specific work-related challenges and broader organizational insight.

10%: Formal or Structured Learning.

Formal learning takes many forms: classrooms, self-paced eLearning, webinars, TED Talks, and podcasts—all of which build foundational skills. McCall, Lombardo, and Eichinger's research concluded that, optimally, only 10 percent of professional development comes from traditional, usually classroom-based, settings. While traditional learning continues to play an important role in workplace education, it often doesn't offer the practical application that learners need to apply new skills. Think of traditional classroom learning as providing the baseline knowledge or how-tos of a new skill, and then leverage mentoring or networking and applying it on the job to fully develop new skills.

If you're wondering what this looks like in practice, consider the following: Julian is a mid-level manager. He has an employee who needs to enhance his *influence* skills. Yet, Julian has a limited training budget. His employee is highly engaged, and Julian wants to encourage his development, so he utilizes the 70/20/10 model to facilitate his learning. He starts by meeting with the employee to brainstorm possibilities:

70/20/10 Framework Example

70%: Experiential Learning	20%: Networking and Mentoring	10%: Traditional Learning
Encourage preparation and practice before the actual conversation or presentation.	Ask a colleague for feedback following a presentation. Be specific in what you ask and focus on its relatability to your influence skills.	Attend a local training organization's class on influence.
Build rapport before you leverage the relationship.	Observe senior leaders who do it well, and then discuss their strategies with them after you observe outstanding influence in action.	Listen to "Leading without Authority" on the LinkedIn Learning channel.
Understand your audience, who they are and what matters to them, and then focus your conversation or presentation on those key messages.		Review "Influencing Others" on Lynda.com

Together, they focused on three learning approaches: understand your audience, observe other leaders, and listen to "Leading without Authority" on LinkedIn Learning. Each strategy came with no cost but allowed the employee to take time within work hours to learn and grow.

Use the 70/20/10 model to broaden your thinking about learning for yourself and your team. The model is a quick-and-easy way to characterize and prioritize development. It isn't meant to be overly prescriptive but to help identify where the most valuable development may come from.

Know When to Coach—and When to Give Feedback

Embedded in effective on-the-job development are coaching, mentoring, and feedback. Effective leaders know the difference and when to use each.

- *Coaching* is an interpersonal-influence process designed to improve performance, develop effective processes, and enhance self-sustaining change.
- *Mentoring*, on the other hand, aims to develop another's career, including developing political savvy, sensitivity to the organization's culture, and proactivity while managing one's own career.
- *Feedback* is an immediate, short interaction that draws attention to a behavior, habit, or style that may get in the way of relationships or productivity—or which may be a strength to leverage.

Both coaching and feedback are outstanding leadership tools that can be used throughout the employee-development process.

Coaching seeks to influence long-term, transformative change. It's not a short-term fix or just-in-time feedback (even though feedback can be an element of coaching). Coaching also proactively addresses potential derailers when considering a person's long-term development aspirations. When someone is moving into a new role, a new team, or a new organizational structure, coaching accelerates their ability to adapt to the team and execute duties effectively. Coaching is also aimed at enhancing and evolving new capabilities over time. Coaching is used only occasionally when employees are developing new skills because, if overused, it can dampen an employee's efforts.

Effective feedback is concise and instructive; it starts a conversation, not a fight. It's a business conversation and is focused on a single issue, not a laundry list of needed corrections. Effective feedback focuses on behavior, not the person; it identifies what "good looks like" and encourages the individual to identify the action he or she will take.

Putting Development into Action

It's great to set the stage for development to happen. It's even more powerful when employees move that intention to action. Look at the simple development plan below. The first column identifies the "what" that an individual plans to develop. These can be interpersonal skills such as influence or collaboration or technical skills such as the month-end close or broadening one's Excel skills. The activities, then, describe the "how": what learning will be undertaken, keeping in mind 70/20/10, to broaden their skills and knowledge. The remainder of the plan helps learners gain greater clarity and insight into their plans.

Result	Activities	Support	Roadblocks	Target Date
What is the desired result or end state that you are trying to develop	What activities such as on-the-job experience, coaching, feedback, and training are you going to undertake to develop this capability?	What support do you need to support your development?	What will prevent you from developing this capability?	What is your target date for developing this capability?

Follow up

Great plans only become great if they turn into action. This is one of the things that separates good managers from great managers—they check in on development over time, make sure employees are progressing on their career goals, and celebrate new insight and learning with each employee.

Conclusion

Learning should and can happen on the job. Highly effective leaders make this happen by creating a climate for learning, ascertaining what each employee needs to learn, and then discovering the best channel to learn that skill. It takes time and effort. Effective leaders create an environment where learning is encouraged by asking team members about new skills and how they were acquired.

They start by assessing each employees' skills and their motivation to engage with their work. Then they consider learning opportunities, knowing that, in fact, the most effective learning happens outside of the classroom and on the job. Finally, they encourage each employee to actively work on an individual-development plan. They encourage development by sharing their own development plan, particularly the areas they would like to improve, thereby creating an atmosphere where everyone is encouraged to learn continuously.

References

1. A brief description of the 70/20/10 learning model. https://www.trainingindustry.com/wiki/content-development/the-702010-model-for-learning-and-development/

Chapter 4

FEEDBACK

MARKETPLACE

Mistake 4: Failure to Take Time to Give and Receive Feedback

You knocked it out of the park! Great job! We couldn't have done it without you! Good work. How often have you heard this from a colleague or boss? Yes, it's great to receive accolades, but how do generalities like these support positive performance? Inexperienced managers often struggle with providing effective feedback, both constructive and for recognition. Why? Because they haven't experienced productive feedback themselves in their own work environment.

Psychometrics, an assessment and research firm focusing on employee engagement, surveyed nearly four hundred Canadian employers and found that 69 percent of the surveyed employees said that they would work harder and feel more engaged if their leaders provided more recognition and praise.[1] This sentiment has been consistent throughout my consulting career. Over the years, I've reviewed dozens of employee engagement surveys within both large and small enterprises. Consistently, "being recognized for a job well done" is one of the lowest-rated items across most organizations.

Giving performance feedback to employees on a regular basis is critical to a manager's success. Effective managers reinforce performance expectations and help employees understand what's going well and what can be done even more effectively. Great feedback doesn't look back to plow old ground; it looks forward to how employees can be even more capable in the work they do.

This challenge is not new. I refer to my own doctoral dissertation. I interviewed recent college graduates to learn about their experience during their first year of full-time employment. Of the nine themes I identified, "lack of feedback" was one of the most prominent.[2] They helped me understand why this was an issue for them. They reminded me that as college students, they received feedback regularly from four to five classes through assignments, papers, and exams. They received multiple instances of feedback numerous times a week. Then they entered the workforce and found "nothing." Many didn't get any feedback in their first six months. When they asked their supervisors, the response was common: "Don't worry, kid, you're doing great. If there's something wrong, I'll let you know. Otherwise, assume everything is okay." This is hardly any insight to work from!

Let's begin with this assumption. The goal of feedback is to help others do things well and meet or exceed expectations. It is *not* to encourage or force your views and perspectives on others. Feedback is a great opportunity to highlight employee strengths and shore up less developed skills. It's an effective way to connect with employees in a personal way and can be utilized to reinforce positive behaviors, develop additional skills, and correct behaviors that may have gotten off track.

Feedback from an Appreciative Perspective

Effective leaders view themselves as talent developers. Talent developers ask individuals to take challenging assignments (while coaching throughout the experience) and encourage all individuals to learn while on the job. Helping others become their best and most effective selves is at least half the job of a manager. Managers constantly observe interactions to see situations where they will be able to give feedback to team members on how to be even more capable in their roles.

Effective feedback often follows an activity or event. Key feedback opportunities might include: during project work, after a formal presentation or deliverable, following key milestones, or during performance discussions (which include quarterly check-ins, performance reviews, and goal setting). *Feedback is effective when it is tied to someone's performance. It focuses on behavior, not personality traits, describes what "good" looks like, is given with sincerity and honesty, and creates a discussion, not an argument.*

Why don't managers give regular feedback? Often, it's because they are afraid that it will backfire—that their feedback might create a defensive reaction, putting at risk a learning opportunity. Therefore, they focus on giving only appreciative feedback. Even when the feedback is about something that didn't go well, it can be discussed in a positive, collaborative way that keeps employees engaged. Appreciative feedback is forward-looking. It asks the individual to consider what can be done differently next time.

Key to engaging in appreciative feedback is asking questions and moving into a future-oriented discussion. Asking questions rather than simply providing statements is a more engaging way to approach feedback. You're literally asking for the employee to share their opinion and perspective of the situation. When this happens, they feel more involved in the discussion, and therefore more committed to the actions moving forward. Asking questions quickly in the conversation avoids stating a "laundry" list of concerns.

Taking a future-focused approach provides a subtle but important shift in tone. Typical feedback is a trudge through past actions. This can feel like scolding—especially when mistakes were made. The shift to future focus is all about the questions you ask.

Ask yourself:
- What did I learn? How will I use this knowledge in the future?
- What changes would I make, given a second chance?
- What would help me do even better next time?

Lastly, appreciative feedback should always include, well, appreciation. The assumption is that most people in most situations really want to do a good job. Challenge yourself to find the good in the situation, regardless of the outcome, and highlight that when sharing feedback. Sharing appreciation can defuse potential tension and clear the way for a healthier discussion focused on opportunities for improvement.

A Simple, Yet Effective Feedback Model
Dozens of feedback models have been created by management consulting firms, academics, and organizations alike. I've utilized many of these and have honed three fine points from them all. Effective feedback:

1. Is *factual;*
2. Describes the *impact* of the behavior; and
3. Is *future-action oriented.*

Effective feedback is concise and instructive; it starts a conversation, not a fight. Jack Zenger is a world expert in the field of leadership development and organizational behavior. He is memorably quoted in a development video on giving constructive feedback that "it shouldn't take you longer than sixty seconds to deliver constructive feedback." This guideline allows the feedback provider to be concise and quickly engage in a conversation about next steps, rather than treading on old ground.

Consider the example below. A manager is providing Lucas feedback following a presentation he delivered:

> "Two executives questioned the accuracy of the report you prepared. There were three instances where the numbers didn't add up. Because of this, they seemed to question the recommendations we provided. What can be done next time to make sure the report is accurate?"

Notice how quickly the manager moves to a question. Why ask a question? It fosters discussion; it also allows the feedback provider and the individual to discuss what happened, offer up additional information, and talk about how it will be different next time.

Effective feedback is usually informal and happens opportunistically. It happens when you find the chance to help others be even more successful. The best leaders are great at giving informal feedback because every situation creates opportunities to elevate the performance of their team. But managers usually refrain from giving feedback, particularly corrective feedback in the moment.

Consider again Lucas from our example above, who prepared for the executive presentation, but due to multiple priorities at home, lost some of the data the morning of the presentation. He used the data he had and hoped he could send updated slides later after he recovered the missing data. With the challenges the executives raised, Lucas most likely knew that the presentation didn't go well. Having his manager step in and urgently demand, "What happened?" only makes matters worse. Effective leaders pause after situations go awry. They make note of what happened and prepare to give feedback at a later date. This pause generally creates an opportunity for a productive, rather than defensive, conversation.

Constructive Feedback Framework

Now, your turn. Use the grid below to draft a feedback message:

Feedback Component	What You Might Say
Includes specifics. What specifically did the person do? What made their actions special or worth noting?	
Describes the impact of the behavior. What difference did their behavior make? What impact did it have on you, others, or the team as a whole?	
Start a conversation to learn more. What question could you ask to learn more about what this person did or how they did it?	

Be Great at Giving Recognition

This same framework works for recognition. How do you move beyond "great job" to something meaningful to the employee? Start by regularly observing your team or colleagues. Capture people doing things right. After all, nearly every employee does way more things right than wrong.

I recall a practice that I learned early in my career. I earned my undergraduate degree in early childhood education. My program at the University of Wisconsin–Stout encouraged us to keep "anecdotal records" of the children in our care as they interacted with their environment and each other. We learned to keep scraps of paper in our pockets to write down observations about and utterances from the children. For example, "Jessica counted to eight while she was staking blocks today, March 14." I stuffed all these scraps into a jar until it was time to write progress reviews for each child. Parents were so pleased to hear these many experiences that had been captured over the months about their children. And, teachers could see progress, or lack of progress, in terms of developmental milestones. It was a practice I've maintained to this day.

I now capture these observations on my cell phone. Now I'm observing adults or college students rather than children, but I've stayed committed to capturing intermittent experiences of when things are going well. For instance, "Mia delivered the report to the executives with presence and handled concerns and objectives with data and insight," or "Leo summarized data from four different reports into a single document and shared it with the team after we struggled to make sense of the all the information that we had gathered." Keeping short notes for each employee on an ongoing basis ensures that you have a full picture of their performance and are not just focusing on the most recent behavior, good or bad.

So how do you deliver effective recognition? Use the same framework!

- Includes *specifics*
- Describes the *impact*
- *Starts a conversation* to learn more

Effective feedback could sound like this:

"The presentation you gave was very effective. Several executives took notes, and two followed up with me to say it was concise yet gave them a lot to consider. How were you able to get all the data we reviewed into such a crisp format?"

Imagine the conversation that could ensue following this feedback! The manager might learn who else was involved in the effort that also needs recognition. They may discover "hidden talents" the employee possesses that could be further leveraged. The manager may discover that while the effort looked "easy," the employee spent countless hours on the presentation and could use additional support next time. Imagine how this discussion could foster trust and build relationships—and it may not take more than a few minutes to happen.

Recognition Feedback Example

Feedback Component	What You Might Say
Includes specifics. What specifically did the person do? What made their actions special or worth noting?	
Describes the impact of the behavior. What difference did their behavior make? What impact did it have on you, others, or the team as a whole?	
Start a conversation to learn more. What question could you ask to learn more about what this person did or how they did it?	

There are countless team members deserving recognition. Take a moment to craft a recognition message for one of them and deliver it right after you finish this chapter!

Keys to Giving Effective Feedback

While no feedback conversation is ever perfect, consider the following guideline to get the most out of a feedback discussion:

- **In-person is better than on the phone.** Non-verbal movements matter in feedback conversations. For distanced employees, connect via video call so people can see each other.
- **Establish relationships before giving constructive feedback.** Feedback goes better if there is an established relationship because trust has already been built. For new employees, if possible, hold off on constructive feedback until you have a few months of interaction between you.
- **Provide timely feedback.** Take time to provide feedback, constructive or recognition, within a few days of the event or behavior. While the content may be difficult to discuss, waiting two

weeks feels disingenuous to those receiving the feedback. Schedule a time to provide the feedback and then deliver it.

- **Base feedback on firsthand accounts.** Gather additional perspective or information if needed, but make sure feedback is based on firsthand knowledge and observation, not what others heard or saw.
- **End with support and affirmation.** Even difficult feedback discussions can foster longer-term relationships. End the conversation by affirming your support for the individual.

Feedback vs. Coaching

Is sharing feedback the same thing as coaching? Not quite. Feedback and coaching are highly related but different. The easiest way to think about the differences between the two is that feedback is about bringing an issue to the person's attention with hopes of a different outcome or different behavior next time. Coaching facilitates discussions driven by the individual, the coachee, not the manager. When giving feedback, the expectation is that you, as a manager, have a firm understanding of what good performance looks like and that you are trying to help the employee achieve that by providing your insights to help them learn.

A good coach asks questions to help an individual gain insights and is not directive in his or her solutions. Coaching and feedback aren't exclusive; feedback can lead to coaching opportunities, and coaching discussions often involve providing feedback.

Develop a Habit of Seeking Feedback Yourself

High-performing managers are more aware of their own strengths and shortcomings than average-performing managers. This awareness helps them to work within what they know they can do to achieve the results they need to achieve. They aren't striving for what they are not.

Allan Church informed our thinking on self-awareness in his groundbreaking research published in an article in 1997.[3] He compared data between self-reports and subordinates on over 1,300 leaders from four independent and varied organizations. He discovered that regardless of the nature of the leader's profession, higher-performing leaders were more aware of their own strengths and shortcomings than their average-performing counterparts. How do they have this understanding? They regularly seek feedback on their own performance and approach.

As a manager, develop a habit for seeking feedback from others: peers, your boss, or even your direct reports. However, approaching a colleague with "how am I doing" or "what did you think?" may not provide actionable insights that you seek. Whether you request feedback via email, phone call, or in a face-to-face meeting, focus on looking forward and getting to specifics. You might ask:

- What did I do that helped our success?
- What could I do even better to be more effective? (Not only asking for "how it went" but about what skills you used.)
- What might I do instead?

You can also share your development focus. For example, you may be working on your influencing skills. Ask your colleague what they have noticed about how you influence and ask for ideas to be a more effective influencer. While your colleague is giving you feedback, take notes. Taking notes shows that you are interested and respectful of your colleague's time. If you are unclear, ask questions for clarifications or for examples.

After gathering the feedback, weigh the pros and cons of what you heard. You don't have to take action on all feedback received. When you do, however, let others know so that they know you valued the time they invested in you.

One new manager reminded me how vital this is. "It's so important to establish a culture for feedback within the group for everyone," said Javier. He went on to explain, "My boss has *never* asked me for feedback on himself or how he engages me or the team or how he can do things better, not once." Javier explained that his boss is completely comfortable sharing feedback on his team's performance, but because he has never asked for feedback in return, everyone feels uncomfortable offering any. He presents an attitude of, "I'm your boss and will give you feedback, but I don't value your opinion and am not personally receptive to it." With an attitude like that, it's impossible to establish a climate for feedback between anyone.

Conclusion

Giving effective feedback is embodied in the capabilities of a highly effective athletic coach. My husband, a middle-school English teacher, coached football for six nearly undefeated seasons. I asked him how he was so successful when our high school team usually faired far worse. "It's about teaching the fundamentals and correcting them when they aren't doing them right. It's knowing what good looks like. To tackle successfully, for example, you need to look at the chest, not in the eyes, then wrap your arms fully around the runner and lower your shoulder to take him down."

Our son, as well as several of his friends, were on my husband's team for a couple of years. As I'd drive them around to various activities, they'd complain that "Mr. Polach doesn't let them run enough plays." They said they always focused on drills instead. Boring, they had concluded. Yet, they were winning, I reminded them.

Providing factual feedback that described the impact of the behavior and was future-action oriented, I believe, was key to his success—just as it is to any successful feedback conversation in a business setting.

Giving effective feedback is just one of many aspects that a manager is responsible for. To be effective, it must be forward-looking, and preparation is key. *Utilizing questions throughout the conversation facilitates a discussion rather than an argument while building trust over time.*

References

1. Psychometrics. https://www.psychometrics.com/wp-content/uploads/2015/engagement_study.pdf
2. Polach, J.L (2004). Understanding the Experience of College Graduates During Their First Year of Employment. *Human Resource Development Quarterly* Vol. 5, Issue 1, p. 5 – 23.
3. Allan Church's article on managerial self-awareness. https://www.researchgate.net/publication/14109411_Managerial_self-awareness_in_high-performning_individuals

Chapter 5

COURAGE TO INFLUENCE

Mistake 5: Not Developing Your Power

A manager always reports to a boss; in fact, many of us may report to several. How do we get them to hear us and encourage our ideas, and how do we garner support from them to drive our ideas forward? Fundamentally, this is the definition of influence. Because managers, by the nature of their role, are usually "stuck in the middle," they often report to a leader or leaders who are senior to them; thus, they don't often have the positional power to get everything they need to get business accomplished. However, their ability to influence others is key to their success. Influence for a manager takes many forms: up, down, and sideways. This chapter focuses on how to influence your boss in order to get work done.

Most of us spend more time influencing and persuading than we think. Daniel Pink, the author of six books, has written extensively in one of his earlier books about influence and persuasion.[1] He argued that out of every hour in our workday, an individual can spend as much as 41 percent of their time persuading others to do something or support something. That's about twenty-four minutes in every hour! He suggests that this persuading and influencing requires the other person to give up something of value, such as their attention, time, or effort, in exchange for what you offer. Therefore, your challenge as a manager is to figure out the value equation in what you are asking for. What does the other person, in many cases, your manager, gain by supporting, championing, or engaging in your idea or position?

Successfully influencing occurs by articulating the value of the work of your team—and why that work matters to the larger organization. Influence allows your ideas to get heard and your team to gain credibility. Teams and individuals with higher credibility gain access to more interesting work and often to more resources.

Managers who are effective at influencing others:

- Commit to building rapport with others over time in ways that are wide and deep in the organization while looking for future collaborations;
- Use different influencing tactics for different people;
- Detect opportunities for adjustments, changes, and innovations that build and broaden relationships and foster influence channels;
- Collect both internal and external facts to support their point of view and recommendations;
- Build relationships in advance with key decision-makers before their support is needed; and
- Understand their facts and can answer questions from others in an engaging, non-defensive manner when challenged.

Power is the ability to make happen what you want to happen—or even block the occurrence of what you don't want to happen. Power is influence potential. *Positional power* comes with your title or, in some cases, your reputation. It involves using status, position, or expertise to ensure support and implementation of the desired ideas, initiatives, or outcomes. NOTE: *manipulation* is not considered influence as it employs negative tactics to get what you want.

As a captain in the Marine Corps, I experienced power firsthand. At that time, I was a personnel officer in the reserves and a human resources (HR) generalist in my civilian life. On weekends, I would don my uniform, shine up my captain's bars, and assume the persona of Captain Polach, leader of twenty marines who were responsible for all HR functions in our squadron. Then on Mondays, I'd put on my business suit and sit at my civilian desk and complete all necessary HR functions for my employer in Washington, D.C. I didn't know any more or less from Sunday to Monday but I could get a lot more done as a captain than as a civilian. Why? Because the power structure was different. In the marines, I gave orders and my marines followed. In my civilian role, I made requests of each manager and they decided whether they would comply. As a marine, I had positional power; as a civilian, I had far less.

Rick Miller[2] wrote an excellent article on how individuals can acquire power without having a positional title. Real power, he argued, is about influence, and it increases as we offer support to others. Real power is more about *giving* support than *getting* support. He suggested that power develops over time, through interactions others have with us. It happens by encouraging others, demonstrating competence, and generating enthusiasm for other's ideas.

Influence

Influence, therefore, is the ability to get others to freely endorse or embrace your ideas and initiatives, whether you have power or not. Ethical influence is bilateral. The one seeking to influence another must be open to being influenced. It involves a conversation, a dialogue that acknowledges individual differences and factors in the relationship or environment. Successful influence often involves multiple conversations and utilizes a mixture of techniques. Successful influence usually demonstrates empathy.

Great influencers aren't imposing their views on someone else; they're listening to the concerns of others and connecting those ideas to meet their needs. Finally, influence is directly related to power. The greater the perceived power, most likely, the greater the influence.

There are numerous techniques for influencing, and they are not all created equally, nor do they have the same outcomes. Influence techniques can be grouped into three broad categories: credibility, emotional, and logic. Their use depends, fundamentally, on the relationship and whether the two parties trust each other.

Credibility

Credibility happens when the influencer ethically appeals to others, convincing them of the source's credibility and character. Credibility requires influencers to portray themselves as sources worth listening to. To be effective, an influencer must choose language that is appropriate for the audience and topic, sounding fair and unbiased, and introducing his or her expertise or pedigree. Confidence and poise are critical, and nonverbals, facial expressions, and body language all matter and are a critical part of communicating credibility.

Emotion

Emotional influence involves persuading someone by appealing to their emotions or feelings; it involves garnering commitment from others. Emotional appeals draw concern from the other person, inspire anger, or motivate them to action by appealing to values. Successfully appealing through emotions involves using vivid language, emotional tone, emotion-evoking stories, and implied meanings. Coherence of body language, voice, and message are important to mastering emotional connections because incongruent nonverbals may contradict one's attempt at leveraging the other person's emotions. Here, think politicians or people selling products on television. They appeal to you not because you need that product, but because you will be better off in some way with it rather than without it.

Logic

Appealing through logic involves convincing the other person by using reason. This form of influence involves citing facts, statistics, research, historical or literal analogies, or authorities on the subject. Logical influencing can be developed by using advanced, theoretical, or abstract language, by citing experts or authorities, quotations, informed opinions, and by constructing logical arguments. This method is meant to evoke a rational response ("Oh, that makes sense") in order to influence a decision in a particular direction. Logical influencers use facts and historical examples to reinforce their points of view.

Steps for Influencing Successfully

Start with your boss's perspective.

What matters to her? What does she care about? Is she a people person or an idealist? Does she need details or broad concepts? What might she have to give up to support your idea? More importantly, what does she gain?

Create a compelling rationale.

Having spent time with the questions above, now you can create your persuasive scenario. The key: speak to the other person's perspective. Don't cover what *you* want them to know but what will interest them and, more importantly, compel them to action. Educate them from that perspective, explaining how they will win if you win.

Describe a path forward.

Leaders can be reluctant to support new ideas because it often means more work for them. Create a high-level path or, at a minimum, outline two or three next steps. What conversations must occur next; who else needs to be informed and engaged? What might be the financial impact of the recommendation? Are there sequenced steps that can be considered to avoid significant disruption?

Ask for support.

It is amazing how many conversations happen without asking for what you want. Find out where you stand with your manager before your meeting. If he needs to consider the idea, agree on a follow-up date. If the answer is no, find out why, and then determine what you would need to do to turn the no to a yes.

Influence Planning Grid

What is my boss's perspective?	
What rationale will be compelling to her?	
What is the path forward or next steps?	
What might be her response?	

Building Your Influencing Skills

Influencing others occurs over time, and it is usually not a single conversation. As such, building influence skills takes a commitment to building relationships and skills for the long term. Consider the following ways to build your influence skills:

Commit to building rapport.

Rapport-building takes time, but it's an investment in the future. Get started today by identifying those who should be a top priority for building rapport. Invite them for a virtual web chat. Develop a habit of broadening your network every week. Ask your manager who else you should know or be acquainted with. Great influencers relate well to others. They take an interest in the other person, and they see themselves as equal to the person they are influencing.

Observe others who navigate organizational politics well.

Some individuals are natural at building relationships within organizations and also navigating egos and opinions. Notice their behaviors:

- How do they listen and summarize what they've heard to ensure everyone's perspectives are included?
- When do they speak in the meeting?
- How are they listened to?
- Take notes and observe, and if you have the opportunity, take time to speak to this capable influencer about his or her success strategies.

Broaden your network before you need it.

Great influencers have broad networks. They dig their wells before they are thirsty. Take time to build yours even if you aren't looking for another job. Meet executives in adjacent functions. Take time to have coffee with people you don't know but who have stature in your organization or community. People love to help others. They can't do this, however, if they don't know you.

Prepare, prepare, prepare.

Identify in advance two or three key points in any message or presentation to leadership. What is critical for them to know? What is your call to action? Tune into the senior leader during the meeting. Be prepared to skip straight to the bottom line if asked or if your time gets cut short. If your audience seems restless, veer from your script and ask the leader what he is curious about. Adapt your approach as needed to successfully influence.

Declare a call to action early.

What outcomes do you seek? What behavior do you need to influence? How can you appeal to the "what's in it for me?" What specifically do you need others to do to achieve the outcomes you seek? Keep the end in mind as you consider how you will influence others. Clearly state what you need your audience to do and co-create a solution or next steps together. Then follow up to ensure it happens.

In Summary

What affects your ability to influence? A chapter on influence wouldn't be complete without a nod to inclusion. We tend to influence first the people we are most comfortable with. It's easier to build rapport with people who look like us, act like us, or have similar backgrounds to us. As leaders, we need to ensure we remain open to being inclusive of a diverse set of ideas.

Your reputation depends upon 1) whether others trust you, 2) your demonstrated expertise, and 3) your own personal track record of delivering on time and within budget. Additionally, it includes 4) your relationships, networks, and professional contacts with others over the long term. Finally, your positional power includes 5) the resources you can bring to situations.

To be an effective influencer, you must be clear about your "best outcome." Effective influencers are crystal clear about the result they are trying to achieve. They create an influence plan before they enter into conversations. And, they engage with the relationships they have built prior to the influence situation. Effective influencers know that successful influence occurs by developing relationships and multiple interactions over time.

References

1. Daniel Pink, To Sell is Human, 2012, Riverhead Books
2. Rick Miller, What Is Power Anyway, Forbes, October 25, 2018. https://www.oforbes.com/sites/rickmiller/2018/10/23/what-is-power-really/?sh=62a7ac3642a7

Chapter 6

DO IT DIFFERENTLY

Mistake 6: Sticking with the Status Quo

G reat innovations don't just happen in an instant. They start with a spark and evolve over time. In fact, many innovations never come to fruition, so don't expect to strike oil every time you innovate.

Instead, and more importantly, focus on doing something differently. Try a new technique; listen to your inner voice that's giving you direction. The techniques described below can be used by yourself or with others to create new ways to think about old problems.

I once listened to an amazing conversation between Adam Grant and Simon Sinek on "A Bit of Optimism: A Podcast with Simon Sinek."[1] During their inspiring conversation about research and leadership behavior, they reminded us that great ideas don't just happen. They evolve when a group of people who are committed to something new comes together to work on the idea until it is ready to share. What a great description of innovation!

A UCLA study found that:

- At age five, we engage in creative tasks 98 times a day, we laugh 113 times, and we ask questions 65 times.
- By age forty-four, we engage in creative tasks 2 times a day, laugh 11 times, and ask questions 6 times.

We seem to lose our zest for creativity as life grabs ahold of us. But it doesn't have to be this way. As a new manager, your role will be challenging, and you will get "bogged down" with the day-to-day. But that doesn't mean innovation can't happen. Innovation is something original, redesigned, or improved that creates substantial value and satisfies unmet need. It can be an individual effort, but as a manager, it's far more interesting and rewarding to engage your team in innovative thinking from time to time—and then step back and watch what happens.

Managers who do this well:

- Anticipate opportunities for bigger thinking before crises arise;
- Stay curious about how things work, particularly in dissimilar industries or products;
- Inquire with the team about new and better ways to do their work;
- Stay abreast of changes in their industry or function and share uncovered great ideas with the team;
- Foster a climate where unusual and even wacky ideas are considered and given time; and
- Create a track record for delivering on novel and enhancing ideas for the organization.

Start with a Simple Process

Whether looking for simple solutions or breakthrough thinking, utilizing a simple process for navigation helps everyone understand the journey and work together collectively. Consider the following whenever the team is stuck and needs to come up with something new and out of the ordinary.

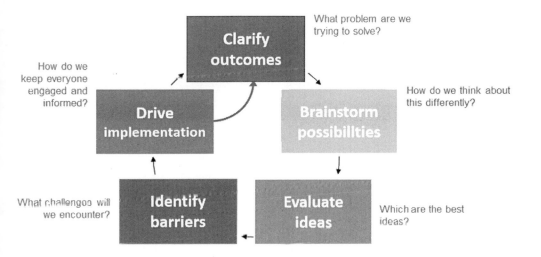

Clarify objectives and outcomes. Start by defining what it is that the team is trying to address. Is it incremental improvement, faster speed, efficiency, or something to beat the competition? If the team doesn't take time to ground themselves in the objective, they may be working towards different ends.

Brainstorm possibilities. I learned long ago from my good friend and author of *The Innovation Equation*, Jacqueline Byrd, that a great way to get idea generation started is by asking the question: How do we think about this differently? This simple question gets ideas flowing. Take time to generate possibilities and avoid the temptation to evaluate, qualify, or dismiss any idea in the idea-generation phase. Is the team still stuck? Utilize one of the innovation techniques outlined below to help your team create something novel in response to a difficult situation—and have fun doing it.

Evaluate ideas. Which are the most promising ideas? Turn to your critical eye and consider the viability of the ideas generated. Start by asking: what has merit in each of these ideas? Are there any that can be combined to create an even better idea? Cull the list down to a couple of ideas that the group is willing to support while solving the identified problem.

Identify barriers. Discuss openly the challenges the team may face in presenting or driving the idea to reality. What are the cost and time constraints? Has the idea been tried before and failed? What circumstances exist that will make it different this time? Who needs to be engaged early for buy-in and support? (See the chapter on influence.)

Drive implementation. Great ideas often get left on the shop floor because the people who created them don't have the passion or perseverance to drive them to implementation. See the chapter on managing change for great ideas to stem resistance and engage stakeholders in the idea's success.

Use Techniques to Create Breakthrough Ideas

Countless books have been written about the innovative process—of particular note are Jacqueline Byrd's *The Innovation Equation* and *Think Like an Innovator.*[2,3] This chapter offers a simple process for innovation with your team and then a number of techniques to use with your team for *developing* innovation when they are stuck or want to think about things in different ways.

Make it worse. Brainstorm solutions by first considering how you could make the problem worse.

1. Write the question on a flipchart.
2. Ask the group, "How could we make it worse? How could it be more *ineffective?*"
3. Now, brainstorm all the "make it worse" strategies and then reflect on true and productive solutions.

Source: Roger von Oech, *Creative Whack Pack,* 2003

Ask why. Take a moment to think deeply about a problem by asking the question "why" five times.

1. Think of the *most* significant problem in the business. Write it down.
2. Now find a partner who also wrote down an idea of the most significant business problem and interview your partner by asking *why* five times.
3. Listen to each response and then ask another *why.*
4. Summarize what you heard after the final *why.*
5. Reverse roles using the same process.
6. Conclude by summarizing insights and "aha's" from the questioning.

Group Prioritize Process. Generate multiple ideas and create a shared priority list.

1. Distribute one 3x5 index card to each participant. Ask them to write their biggest challenge or best idea on the card (only one challenge or idea per card).
2. Ask all participants to stand up and switch their cards with others several times for about one minute so that no one has his or her own card.

3. Now, ask them to find one partner, and between the two individuals, assign seven points across the two cards. The point values are assigned based on which challenge is of a higher or more pressing priority or which idea is stronger. For example, one card can be assigned four points, another three; one card can be assigned two points, the other five.
4. Ask participants to write their agreed-upon point value on each card.
5. Now repeat the process three more times: switch cards for a minute, then find a partner and assign seven points between the two cards.
6. After four full rounds, ask participants to return to their seats.
7. At a flipchart, write down the five or six "top point-getter" challenges or ideas. Because there are four rounds, one card could receive twenty-eight points, but this is highly unlikely.
8. Ask participants to form small groups based on the identified challenges or ideas. Encourage no more than six people per group.

Source: Sardek Love, Infinity Consulting and Training Solutions

See the positive. Brainstorm all the positives about an idea. Instead of taking time to debate the ideas as flawed, focus on what works or the positive aspects of the ideas.

Source: Roger von Oech, *Creative Whack Pack*, 2003

The Secret. Solve a problem by improving on someone else's idea.

1. Write the problem on a flipchart.
2. Without speaking, each person writes down their solution on a *colored* sticky note.
3. Partner by twos and discuss each other's ideas. Find an improvement to each idea.

4. Write all the improved ideas on *different colored sticky notes*. *STOP HERE*.
5. Now find one other pair and review all four ideas.
6. Review each of the revised ideas and find one improvement for each idea. Write them on a *third colored* sticky note (you should have four). *STOP HERE*.
7. As a group, organize the sticky notes by *RISK* and *VALUE*.
8. Select the most promising ideas to move forward with.

	Low Risk	Med Risk	High Risk
Low Value			
Med Value			
High Value			

Source: Jacqueline Byrd, *The Voice of the Innovator*, 2013

Creatrix® Ba. Gather the group for silent brainstorming with only a flipchart and marker; work without talking for thirty to forty-five minutes on solving the problem.

1. Move the team into a circle facing one another. There should be no barriers such as tables, desks, et cetera—just people in a circle.
2. Write a question, challenge, or aim on the flipchart in the middle of the group.
3. The group utilizes *only* one flipchart and one marker.
4. Their objective: in the thirty minutes allotted, develop at least three new ideas—ideas that *no one* has heard of before. As a group, they must come away with at least three brand new ideas to address the aim or challenge.
5. **Note:** No one can talk during this exercise.

Source: Jacqueline Byrd, *The Voice of the Innovator*, 2013

Think about it differently. Identify similarities in dissimilar objectives.

1. Give one group or several teams three different objectives.
2. Each team has a different set of three objectives. These can be printed on flashcards, or you can use three very dissimilar objects.
3. Give the team (or teams) five minutes to list as many similarities they can think of across all three objects.
4. Ask each team to share their list.
   Complete a second round for another seven minutes. Notice how many *new* ways are listed that are similar but different to the ideas identified in round one.

New associations. Find new associations from something dissimilar by selecting random text in a book and then making associations. Open a book at random and put your finger on a word. Read the word out loud and make associations between the word on the page and the problem or challenge at hand. Ask, "How does this word relate to what we are struggling with?"

Source: Roger von Oech, *Creative Whack Pack*, 2003

Associate with nature. Select an animal or plant; think about how it would go about solving the problem. Ask the group to each select a plant or animal from nature. Have them write down what that object would think about the problem at hand. What insights can the group make from these insights?

Source: Roger von Oech, *Creative Whack Pack*, 2003

What's the worst that could happen? Brainstorm all the things that could happen if the solution is implemented poorly or doesn't work. If the group is stuck on how to move forward, ask, "What can go wrong?" Brainstorm all the disasters that might happen. Be wild and inventive.

Spend at least fifteen minutes on this so that all ideas are surfaced. Now evaluate which ones are likely to happen. Create solutions for those.

Think like a kid. Solve the problem by thinking about how a six-year-old would address the challenge. Free up the group's thinking by asking, "How would a kid solve this problem?" Let the ideas flow and have fun!

Leverage silence. Allow participants to listen to their inner voice by turning down the lights and allowing silence to happen. Calm the voice inside your head and let the silence happen. Allow participants ten to fifteen minutes to listen to their inner voices. Check in afterward by asking for input from each participant concerning insights and perspectives. What each participant's inner voice have to say?

Listen to your hunch. Ask everyone to share their hunches about an idea or problem. If the group is stuck, poll everyone on the team by asking, "What is your hunch?" Suspend judgment and the need for more data. Then respond to everyone's best thinking.

Source: Roger von Oech, *Creative Whack Pack*, 2003

Use a Decision Grid. *Deliberately evaluate ideas using a structured grid.* When the group is struggling on how to move forward, chart out the options using the Decision Grid below.

	Low Risk	Med Risk	High Risk
Low Value			
Med Value			
High Value			

Silent mind storming. Silently brainstorm and list twenty solutions to a problem. Turn inward to solve a difficult problem by finding a quiet space. Using a piece of paper and pen, brainstorm solutions to a challenge you are facing by listing twenty solutions. You will get stuck after about eight ideas, but keep going. Push your mind to deliver additional new and unique ideas. Don't stop until you have at least twenty ideas. Your last three or four ideas should be spectacular!

What if . . . Stimulate thinking by asking crazy questions.

1. Tape four or five flipchart papers on the walls around the room, each with a "What if . . ." question at the top, such as "What if we didn't need to sleep at night?" or "What if the sky was green?"
2. Ask people to provide responses to each question around the room.
3. Now ask others to create their own "What if . . ." questions related to the business, like "What if we satisfied every customer?"
4. Answer the questions around the room and use those responses as inspiration for the discussions of the team.
   Source: Jacqueline Byrd, *The Voice of the Innovator*, 2013

Develop Innovating Thinking Skills

Still holding back? An innovation mindset builds over time. Consider the following ways to build your capabilities before you're called upon to generate *big* ideas.

Seek out others who are creative. Big thinkers seldom put their ideas together alone. Observe how others champion and drive issues to implementation.

Practice iterative thinking. No idea or design is perfect the first time. Allow ideas to "ruminate" for periods of time. Share them with others and gain their perspective and ideas.

Work with the information you have. We all wish for more clarity—one more data point, one more analysis, but sometimes, it's just not possible. Look at the information you have in front of you today. What does it say? This is a great time to use your intuition. What does your past experience tell you to do? What's the worst thing that can happen given the limited information you have? Take action and then live with the decision.

Let go of sureness. In chaos, our immediate reaction is to gain clarity. Suspend that tendency. Work with what you know. Find opportunity in what is not clear. Extend grace and patience to others who are struggling. Work with the information you have rather than the information you wish you had.

Check your perspective with others. We often think that we need to go through hardship alone. What are others saying? How are they coping? Is there someone available to check your point of view? You will find you aren't alone. Take time to check in with others on how they are managing and to gain insight from their perspectives.

We all have the power and capability to be more innovative. Letting go of the notion that great ideas just pop into our heads is the first step. Then collaborate with others to identify what's possible, which might even be hidden because the team hasn't taken the time to explore. Finally, take time with your team to be innovative—to think *big*. It won't happen in your day-to-day work life because your mind is filled with pressing tasks and issues. Start with the simple question, "How can we do this differently," and then see what happens.

Conclusion

Innovative thinking *is* part of your job as a manager. This chapter isn't intended to make you a breakthrough thinker. It provides you with an innovative process that you can use by yourself or with your team, and then it offers up over a dozen innovative techniques to try with your team when they are stuck—stuck on a lack of solutions, stuck on processes that don't work, stuck on doing things the same old way. Let go of sureness and pick one or two techniques with your team when solutions are evasive. Make time for *big* thinking. Have fun and be delighted with what emerges.

References

1. *A Bit of Optimism: A Podcast with Simon Sinek.* https://simonkinek.com/discover/episode-17-a-bit-of-everything-with-adam-grant/
2. Jacqueline Byrd. *The Innovation Equation: Building Creativity and Risk-taking in Your Organization.* 2002, Pheiffer.
3. Jacqueline Byrd. *The Voice of the Innovator.* https://www.voiceoftheinnovator.com

Chapter 7

MAKE CHANGE STICK

Mistake 7: Not Getting Ahead of Change

Recently I worked with a senior team at a mid-sized, growing enterprise. They were trying to get ahead of market pressures: new technology was being installed across multiple departments, shop floors were expanding to streamline the production processes, and new products were being introduced to edge out the competition. More daunting—all this change was occurring simultaneously!

New or inexperienced managers often struggle with managing change because they have rarely led a successful change initiative themselves. They don't have a model or framework to follow, and managing change is hard work. Traditional change models no longer apply. Organizations aren't static entities with time to freeze, unfreeze, and refreeze, as author Kurt Lewin suggested in his 1951 book, *Field Theory in Social Science.*[1] Even the easily understood framework of William Bridges,[2] author of *The Way of Transition: Embracing Life's Most Difficult Moments*—a framework of endings and beginnings with an awkward neutral zone in the middle—no longer speaks to the dynamic and continuous nature of change we face in organizations today. These methodologies all suggested that something dramatic was going to happen, chaos would ensue, and then the organization would land in a calmer and, indeed, better place.

That isn't reality because today's organizations are involved in constant, multiple, and simultaneous changes. Rather than thinking about change as an event, experienced and highly effective leaders think about change as a constant, and they have built the habits of managing change into their daily work routines. Thinking like a boss requires you to constantly scan for change on the horizon—and get ahead of it before it creates chaos, confusion, and unrest within the workforce. As one wise leader said to me, "If it isn't broken, keep fixing it so it doesn't break."

Challenges Managing Change

Leaders need to anticipate, plan for, and manage the change and transition process. Managing change is interactive and ongoing—not a single activity. If managed well, change can be an engaging activity for the team, one that builds trust and commitment to a better new. However, if dealt with poorly, it can cause frustration, anxiety, and lower productivity—and even lead to burnout.

When employees are not given enough information, they are reluctant to support and enable change. Change in process, procedures, or businesses often stall or swirl. Employees bring rumors to the surface and rehash decisions. If not managed well, change can be reactionary. Staff find out about changes "just in time," rather than in advance, and as such, feel ill-prepared to accept and adapt to the change. This can result in employees appearing to be *change-resistant.*

Consider Mark, for example. Mark had been promoted from his peer group just three months ago in an insurance call center. Like all employees in the center, he had watched productivity numbers sink as new software was introduced. When he had checked in with his manager a few weeks prior, the manager had said not to worry about it, that the call center was in transition and that things would settle down over time. Mark was stunned when he came to work the next Monday to read a scathing warning from his vice president that teams had two weeks to return productivity numbers to pre-system implementation levels or "more drastic actions" would be taken. Mark shared the news with his staff, who were shocked and angered. They spent the day discussing potential "more drastic actions" rather than focusing on how to address the issues. Mark failed to get ahead of change.

Leaders who manage change well:

- Explain the "why" as well as creating the "what" of change;
- Create a complete and detailed change plan and share it with staff and other stakeholders;
- Facilitate an open and trusting process for team members to ask questions and share anxieties;
- Look for early wins and celebrate them broadly;
- Encourage negative emotions to be recognized, addressed, and managed;
- Appreciate the pace of change and are on the lookout for change fatigue among staff; and
- Share negative information with compassion and care.

A Simple Change Process

How do you think like a successful boss about change? It starts by adopting and utilizing a change process, which is key to effectively managing change. Change processes and methodologies abound. Major consulting firms such as Deloitte, E&Y, and KPMG have had structured change processes for years. Smaller firms like ProSci offer tools and certifications in their approach.[3]

If you need something simple and quick, consider the following steps in planning for and implementing a successful change initiative. I've evolved this model over the years. The beauty of the model is that it works for both small changes such as reorganizing departmental roles and for major changes such as implementing a new performance-management system across the entire enterprise. The model, fashioned from the classic leading-change model introduced by John Kotter, author of *Leading Change*,[4] allows the manager or change-management practitioner to think logically through the change before it is shared with various employee groups and other stakeholders.

1	2	3	4	5
Craft a Compelling VISION	Identify STAKEHOLDERS & assess impact	Build new SYSTEMS & Launch QUICK WINS	COMMUNICATE the change	Imbed in the CULTURE

1. Craft a compelling vision. New managers often forget this step. Most managers, even when not intimately involved in the planning of the change, are usually given a "heads up" early on so that they have had time to become familiar with and think about the change. However, employees are often given less lead time to prepare for change. Mark had an inkling of productivity issues in his call center, yet he failed to act. Whether the boss creates a call for action or not, effective leaders scan the horizon for change and begin to prepare before a crisis arises. Regardless of whether they are to spearhead the change or lead a group that is impacted by the change, highly effective leaders start by crafting a compelling vision for the change that includes:

- What will change?
- What won't change?
- What are the benefits of the change to those impacted?
- How might others react?

This is not a ten-minute activity. Careful consideration must be given to each question, and conversations should be held with people closer to the change. After considering these characteristics, craft a simple vision that can be shared in five minutes or less with the team and others. Share drafts of your vision with one or two team members. Get their reactions and adjust your vision based on their feedback. This is a great way to garner early buy-in.

2. Identify stakeholders and assess the impact. Not all stakeholders are affected equally. Focus on the ones that will be most impacted by the change and those who, if managed poorly, might have the greatest negative impact if the change is not being sustained. A stakeholder group can be one person or hundreds. Members of a stakeholder group have similar jobs or responsibilities, so they can be managed as a group to streamline communication. Put yourself in the shoes of each stakeholder group. Identify how they might be impacted by the change.

Ask yourself the following:

- What do I want them to *know* about the change?
- What do I want them to believe or *feel* about the change?
- What actions do I need them to take or *do* in making the change successful?

The KNOW/FEEL/DO model grew out of the 1990s when change-management practitioners were coming to grips with the complexity of change and the impact of change upon various employee groups. This simple model allows the manager to look at the change's impact from multiple perspectives. While a manager can't judge for certain how stakeholders will *feel* about a change, a manager can help them understand the change and then drive them to productive action.

These first two steps are critical to getting ahead of change successfully. Imagine if Mark had taken the time to complete these two steps immediately after he had raised concerns with his boss. 1) He would have searched through old emails looking for communications about the systems changes and captured the *what* and *why* from them to craft a vision for his team. 2) Then he would have assessed the impact to his call-center employees and any other key stakeholders who might not have been his direct reports but who had key responsibilities in making the change stick. If he had completed these two steps, he would have been ready to engage his team when the difficult edict from senior management had been issued.

3. **Build new systems and processes and launch quick wins.** This is where the heavy lifting of the change happens. In this step, processes are redesigned, procedures are written, and implementation timelines are crafted. As you work through this step, consider the following:

- What is the anticipated improved outcome from this change, and how will it be measured?
- How can the new process or procedures be broken down into quick wins? What should be implemented first for the most value?
- What can be done quickly to generate an immediate improvement and faith in the larger change?
- How should the team be educated or trained to ensure understanding and compliance?
- How could rewards or recognition be used to celebrate achieving short-term goals and quick wins?

4. **Communicate the change.** After completing steps one through three, the hard work has been completed. The task now is to "sell" the change in a compelling and understandable manner.

The **4-P framework** can act as a blueprint for communication:

- **Purpose**: Why are we doing this, and what is the anticipated improved outcome? The vision created in Step 1 informs this content.
- **Picture**: What will the future look like? How will the process differ from today, and what will be measured and valued?
- **Plan:** What is the path forward? What is the timeline? Who will be trained and when? What happens to individuals who struggle with the new way of doing things?
- **Participate**: How can others become involved and support the change's success?

5. Embed the change in the culture. Change, no matter how well planned and executed, does not necessarily sustain itself unless it is embedded into long-term systems in the organization. Effective leaders consider how the change will be sustained before launching the change. They determine how the changed behaviors will be reinforced and how to keep the change at the top of employees' minds so that they don't slip into old and familiar habits. Consider:

- How do we ensure that this change sustains itself?
- What additional training or education might be needed?
- What recognition and celebrations need to happen?
- Does the current organization structure support the new processes?

This simple yet effective change model outlined above can provide a framework for both major and minor changes. Effective leaders use this process every time a change presents itself in order to ensure that the change is completely thought through, stakeholders are engaged, and communication happens.

A Bit More About Stakeholders

As I mentioned before, not all stakeholder groups are affected equally. Some need to be managed more carefully than others. Start by identifying each stakeholder group: leaders, managers, and frontline employees in various functions. Stakeholders can consist of one or hundreds. Identify the group, how they might be impacted, and roughly how many people are in the stakeholder group. Be sure to consider both internal *and* external stakeholders such as customers or suppliers. Identify how significant the change's impact will be for each group. Some groups may require only small changes to work processes, while others may experience major work redesign. This analysis lays the foundation for identifying the activities needed to help others move successfully through the change.

Multiple stakeholders often require multiple communication channels. Start by understanding existing communication channels. How does the stakeholder group currently receive and share information? Is there an internal web portal? Instant messaging? A regularly scheduled newsletter?

Stakeholder groups need information in advance of the change launch, and they need opportunities to ask questions and gain clarity. It is human nature to be concerned about change; we wonder, we worry, yet often with major changes, most things remain the same. Take the time to define and communicate not only what *will change* but also *what will stay the same.* If you're not clear about what might change when discussing the change with your team, say so, and then share a date when you'll have an update. Remember, this is the time to repeat the same message multiple times. It doesn't mean people aren't interested; it usually means they are busy with other things and haven't engaged yet.

Timeworn Tactics for Leading Change

I've helped dozens of large and small organizations implement change. It isn't easy, and there's always more that can be done. I helped a particular health insurance provider implement a career-development-

and-competency model for its entire organization of over two hundred thousand employees. As we approached the implementation to the entire workforce, the project's leader was receiving numerous questions from senior leaders about whether we had fully prepared senior and mid-level leaders to support their employees in engaging with the resources that had been created.

Our team took the time to capture the various readiness actions that we had already taken: 1) training to managers, 2) senior-leader communications, 3) a self-paced learning portal with multiple printed and video resources to support the step-by-step process, 4) change champions across the enterprise who were early adopters, 5) multiple discussions with HR leadership teams to equip them with supporting their leaders, and 6) measurement strategies to track engagement.

We were surprised at how many activities and resources we had built. The great insight was that not all resources and activities were on the initial change plan. Many were opportunistic! We were invited to a senior-leader meeting to discuss the new resources. Another time, a leader discussed the change in his regular monthly communication. Change happens both organically and inorganically, and wise leaders leverage both.

There are numerous strategies for managing change, and many have been covered above. Below are a number of tactics that could be incorporated into any change program, large or small. They are based on collective years of experience leading change and are time-tested, dependable, and make a difference. They are simple, easy to incorporate, and can make a change effort successful.

1. **Fully engage managers and supervisors early and often.** Educate and equip them to engage their staff. "Our attitude is everything," a wise sage reminded me. Engage employees fully so that they can get on board to support and lead the change.

2. **Be patient.** Executives are always ahead of the curve; they need to be reminded, however, to allow their organizations to catch up. It takes time to learn new skills and accept new ways of

thinking. We all learn at different rates. When others are slow to adopt a change, it does not mean that they don't like the change, it usually means that they need time to understand it, embrace it, and learn the newly required skills.

3. **Create a "sounding board" to ascertain buy-in, understanding, and commitment.** Sounding boards are groups of employees who are closely connected to the change. They become early adopters and advocates for the change. Sounding board members should be carefully selected by the organization; they are informal leaders who others trust and hold in high regard. Guidelines for establishing a successful sounding board can be requested from *janetpolach@yahoo.com.*

4. **Brand the change initiative.** While not critical, giving the change a name and identity is a useful tactic. The organization's marketing group can assist with this task in a cost-effective way. Giving the initiative a look and feel can help people anchor their perspectives and fit initiatives together. However, avoid going overboard. A color scheme and logo are adequate, but grand efforts can lead employees to disparage the effort and lose focus on the message of the change.

5. **Leverage what already works by incorporating existing patterns and methods of communicating.** Avoid launching a new newsletter or website that employees have to find, read, or deal with. Leverage channels that already exist—all-hands meetings, manager meetings, regular email communication, traditional bulletin boards. Identify dependable and easy-to-administer communication channels and share information on a regular and consistent basis.

6. **Engage others in the change process.** Change isn't a solo sport, so engage others in the journey. Volunteer to work on a change initiative, even if you are not leading it. Network with multiple individuals inside (and outside) your organization to learn from

others who have led large change initiatives. Identify what's been consistent in their experiences and what they've learned.

7. **Scan the horizon.** Half the battle with managing change is getting ahead of it before it happens. Adopt the habit of scanning the environment regularly for change. What are the markets doing? Is hiring happening, or is there a hiring freeze? What is the competition doing? Some great "trends to watch" sites are www.wundermanthompson.com, www.businessnewsdaily.com, www.thebalancesmb.com, and www.entrepreneur.com.

8. **Learn about managing change.** Dozens of books and hundreds of articles have been written about leading change. Equip yourself now. Read, listen to podcasts, or even get certified. There are classics like John Kotter's *Leading Change* (www.kotter-inc.com) and structured methodologies like ProSci (www.prosci.com). Find a process that fits you, and then follow it.

Summary

Change in organizations is persistent and perpetual. While change is often triggered by an event such as a merger or a system implementation, it needs to be embraced as a constant because each new change must fit within other existing and ongoing changes. Thinking like a boss includes earnestly accepting change and building change practices into your everyday work life.

Utilize the tools in this chapter. Engage your team early in the process, and then use the process outlined to set the stage for new and innovative thinking. Leverage one or more of the problem-solving tools presented here to create breakthrough ideas and drive them to implementation. Then communicate, communicate, communicate. Change can't be overcommunicated enough! Share information with your team, and then make time for questions and concerns. Know that you don't have to have all the answers, particularly when the change is imposed upon your group, but you can create a climate where team members feel comfortable asking difficult questions and are patient enough to wait for answers.

References

1. Lewin, K., (1951). *Field Theory in Social Science*, New York: Harper & Row.
2. Bridges, W., (2001). *The Way of Transition: Embracing Life's Most Difficult Moments.* Cambridge, MA: Da Capo Press
3. https://www.proscie.com
4. Kotter, J. (2012). *Leading Change.* Cambridge, MA: Harvard Business Review Press.

Chapter 8

BECOMING THE LEADER THAT IS IN YOU

While you've reached the end of this guide, you may be just beginning your leadership journey. I've been fortunate to coach young frontline leaders as well as highly experienced senior leaders. For most leaders, roles expand and evolve over time. The requirements for leaders and their work are constantly evolving, so they must learn and utilize different skills and gain new perspectives. So, being an effective leader is a journey, not an end state.

Demonstrate Vitality

Resiliency is key to surviving a leader's first year. Demands change as a manager. As an individual contributor, you were responsible to your team, but they didn't necessarily set expectations on your time. As a manager, you are responsible to not only your team but also to your manager. Managing these myriad demands requires stamina and self-care.

Vitality, the state of being strong and active, is a great word to describe what effective leaders achieve when they are deliberate about resiliency and self-care. They use strategies and approaches for allocating and spending time their time deliberately, and they create personal guidelines for identifying energizing activities to keep themselves engaged and committed in work and life.

The key to vitality starts with healthy habits:

- Embrace a mindset that encourages you to do what you want to do, not because you have to do it.
- Get a good night's sleep and eat a good breakfast to give yourself more energy during the day.
- Do something physically vigorous in the morning (e.g., go for a run, do power yoga, jump on a mini-trampoline, do an exercise video).
- Go out of your way to become more involved in an organization to which you already belong.
- Find passion in what you're doing.

Assess Your Vitality

Not sure if you are balanced in all aspects of your life? The Life-Wheel can give you a quick-and-easy snapshot.

Utilize the diagram below. First, plot your "ideal" style with an X. Where would you prefer your life to be in each of the areas? Connect the dots to form an enclosed shape.

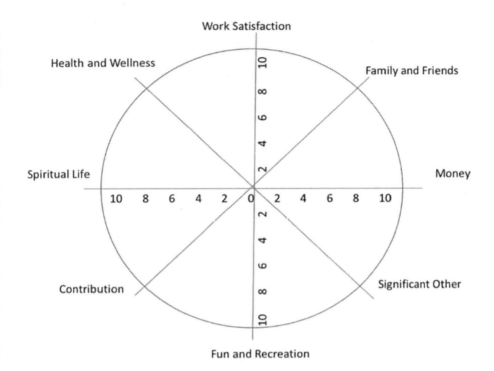

Now, plot with a different symbol where you are currently. Then connect the dots to form an enclosed shape. What do you notice? Keep in mind, your ideal doesn't have to be a ten for all dimensions. Perhaps money isn't a motivator, so currently, you may be a six.

Life-Wheel Reflection	Your Responses
What delights you about the shape above?	
What concerns you the most?	
What actions might you take based on this reflection?	

Much has been written on vitality, resilience, mindfulness management, and wellbeing. While there's too many to list here, you are encouraged to find a great book or podcast on tips for maintaining your vitality and then commit to one or two tactics over the long term.

Know Yourself Better in Order to Lead Others Better

When you think like the boss, you know that not everyone receives your information in the same way. Our upbringing, education, and experiences inform how we take in information, be it written or verbal. So, effective managers know that they need to adapt their style to difficult individuals.

But how do you know a stakeholder's preferred style and how they best receive incoming information? Well, you could ask them, but they may not be able to articulate it clearly. Most people "know it when they see it."

Carl Gustav Jung was a Swiss psychiatrist and psychoanalyst who founded the field of analytical psychology, the lifelong psychological process of differentiating the self out of each individual's conscious and unconscious elements.[1]

Jung considered it to be the main task of human development. He created some of the best-known psychological concepts, including synchronicity, the collective unconsciousness, archetypal phenomena, and extraversion and introversion. While archetypes first appeared in Plato's writing, Carl Jung has been generally given credit for introducing archetypes to the world in human development because they help ground us in patterns that provide cues to understanding another's behaviors.

Dozens of archetype models (MBTI, Enneagram, DiSC, Insights Discovery, Team Dimensions, etc.) have been created out of Jung's initial work on personality type. They are useful in helping us understand how and why others interact so differently than we do. These assessments are self-report questionnaires that indicate differing psychological preferences in how people perceive and interact with their world, what criteria they use to make decisions, and under what circumstances they decide to act.[2]

I find Insights Discovery[3] particularly useful because of its simplicity. The assessment considers just two dimensions: how people gain energy in their interactions with others and under what criteria do individuals make decisions. Insights Discovery then turns these preferences into a simple-yet-memorable four-color model that helps people understand their style, their blind spots, and the value they bring to others on a team.

The vertical axis describes where you *get your energy*. Are you extroverted or introverted? Do you get your energy and become recharged by interacting with others and by group problem-solving? Or do you recharge in the quiet of your own mind, preferring to find solutions first and then share them with others?

The horizontal axis focuses on *decision-making*. Under what criteria do you decide? Do you make decisions with the facts and details, or do you decide with people in mind? Do you decide with your head or your heart?

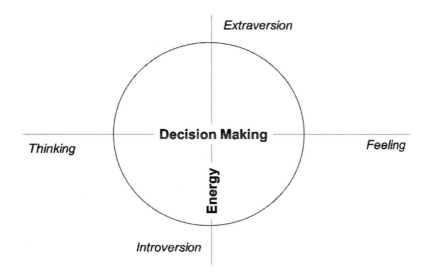

Insights Discovery then creates a colorful visual depiction of the model to help people understand and remember. In a workshop, the team completes the assessment beforehand, then discusses the strengths and blind spots of each profile. They gain appreciation for how others see the world, which helps build relationships.

I've used this tool with countless groups, including, for example, engineers, spiritual leaders, and healthcare-delivery leaders. They find that it offers great insight in understanding their own preferences, but more importantly, in understanding the preferences of their coworkers. Said one individual when she suddenly learned to appreciate a colleague, "She wasn't being difficult or challenging me, she was just trying to understand through data and detail so she could support my point of view!"

There are many ways to get to the same result. Orient on how others best receive information. Use the information and perspective above to consider how you might communicate effectively with others on your team and with your boss.

For those who lead with:

- **Extroverts.** Let them talk it out. Plan to take time to problem-solve in the moment rather than within emails. Allow extroverts to build on other people's ideas, but recognize that they have a tendency to take over the conversation, and find ways to allow others who are more reserved to also enter into the conversation.

- **Introverts.** They need to think it through. Provide them background material before meetings so that they can start their processing ahead of others. Call on them in-meeting to make sure their ideas are also heard. Thank them privately for their hard work and their insight. True introverts generally don't appreciate public recognition.

- **Thinkers.** These individuals are focused on *fairness for all*, and they use data and precedent to make decisions. They want to treat everyone equally, regardless of circumstances—so they may struggle with making exceptions. Pair them with someone who will consider others' reactions and feelings before communicating.

- **Feelers.** These individuals tend to make decisions from their heart, striving for harmony and inclusion. They like to gain consensus, knowing that taking the time to do so will create more buy-in and acceptance, particularly of unpopular decisions. They may become delayed in making tough decisions because of the potential impact on others—so establish timelines for decisions and communications.

There are multiple personality inventories and style assessments on the market. Choose one that resonates with you. Utilize a skilled facilitator to introduce these concepts to your team. Leverage others' strengths in problem-solving or during team meetings to help the team move through difficult topics.

Ask for Help Before You Need It

One of the most significant mistakes new managers make *is thinking they can go it alone.* Instead, ask for help before you need it. Don't be afraid to get perspective from others you trust as you grow as a new manager. Find a mentor or mentors. Mentors help us navigate through internal politics. Seek out individuals not in your direct chain of command who care about you and your success. Find a mentor before you need one. Establish the relationship and invite their advice and counsel.

I'm recalling a mentoring relationship that was established quite serendipitously with a recent client. I was on a long-term project when Rick and I struck up a friendship—that extra time turned into a two-way mentorship. Yes, two-way! Sometimes we think that mentoring is only one way—the mentor supporting the mentee. But ask any mentor, and they will say that they learned as much from their mentee as they believe the mentee learned from them!

Rick and I had the opportunity to work on a couple of projects together, and over time, he sought out advice and insight from me on career decisions and internal politics. I think our relationship was so powerful because we come from different generations. He offers me insight in the use of technology and perspectives from individuals on the upward slope of their careers. I offer insight from the many organizations I've worked with and perspectives from the other half of my career. He agreed to partner with me, mentoring and giving me his insights in writing this book. While Rick and I don't work as closely together now, we have formed a lasting bond. We may now go for months without connecting, but like any good relationship, we pick up where we left off.

A mentor or mentors are invaluable to your career success. They may reside inside or outside the organization. They are valuable for testing your thinking, particularly when you have less experience, and they can help you avoid making emotional or weak decisions.

Engage in Self-Reflection

Knowing yourself, including faults, blind spots, or overused strengths are important as you work with your team. High-performing managers are more aware of their own strengths and shortcomings than average-performing managers. This awareness helps them to work within what they know they can do in order to achieve the results they need to achieve. They aren't striving for what they are not. Allan Church informed our thinking on self-awareness in his groundbreaking research published in 1997.[4] He compared data between self-reports and subordinates of over 1,300 leaders from four independent and varied organizations. He discovered that regardless of the nature of the leader's profession, higher-performing leaders were more aware of their own strengths and shortcomings than their average-performing counterparts. How did they have this understanding? They regularly sought out feedback on their own performance and approach.

As pointed out in a previous chapter that as a manager, one should develop a habit for seeking feedback from others, peers, your boss—even your direct reports. Approaching a colleague with "how am I doing" or "what did you think?" may not provide actionable insights that you seek. Whether you request feedback via email, phone call, or a face-to-face meeting, focus on looking forward and getting to specifics.

Ask yourself:

- What did I do that helped our success?
- What could I do even better to be more effective? Ask not only "how it went" but what skills did you use.
- What might I do instead?
- How else can I help you be successful?

After gathering the feedback, weigh the pros and cons of what you heard. You don't have to take action on all feedback received. When you do take actions, however, let others know so that they can appreciate the time they've invested in you. Turn other's input into action by creating a development plan and reviewing it regularly.

Share Your Development Focus with Your Staff

Highly effective leaders work on their own development continuously. They see their success as an evolving journey of learning and growing, hitting plateaus, meet new challenges, and then gaining new insights as they continue to evolve. When you think like a boss, you share your learning journey regularly with your staff. You share with them where you're struggling and how you are approaching resolution. You share what you've learned and what you're doing differently because of it.

A number of years ago, I created a highly effective leadership-development program for an organization's general managers. It was a highly interactive, multi-day program that allowed leaders to evolve their leadership presence and personality over a year's time. I struggled with how to conclude the program with a significant experience that didn't turn out to be more hype than substance. On a long forty-mile bike ride on a 90-degree day on a Wisconsin county road, it came to me: a letter to my staff. I've used this simple yet powerful framework in most programs ever since. It allows the leader to reflect on his learning and to deliberately share that learning with his staff.

Whenever you undergo a significant learning experience, whether it be informally through a stretch assignment or formally through a leadership program, you are changed. You've taken time away from your staff to engage in learning, and I believe that you owe your staff a reflection on what you discovered.

Start with a simple reflection:

- What did I learn about myself?
- What am I trying to do differently?
- How did others help me?

Then incorporate these new insights into your daily routines. Take time at the end of the week to reflect on what worked and what you need to continue to focus on.

The Transition to Manager

We considered the following model in the first chapter when we highlighted the dramatic transition from individual contributor to front-line manager. Myriad leaders have successfully made the transition, but just as many have struggled.

Managers
- Plan
- Execute
- Communicate
- Develop others

Individual Contributors
- Understand responsibilities
- Execute tasks
- Report progress
- Learn and grow

During the transition from individual contributor to manager, some but not all skills and capabilities are discarded, while others are required and must be developed.

The work of the manager differs from the work of the individual contributor in significant ways. First, managers have a larger scope and more complex responsibilities. They have broader decision-making responsibilities, and they impact the organization at a higher level than do individual contributors. Managers are responsible for accomplishing the organization's strategies and delivering on the quarter's plan. Fundamentally, they get things done through others.

Set Your Intention

We've covered a lot of ground in this short book. We identified the difference between an individual contributor and manager, we discussed planning and execution, and we talked about the value of effective feedback and how to give it. We discussed influence, and we provided a framework for managing change. Obviously, you can't do all of this well at once. Skills come with time and practice. So, set a focus for your work as a leader. What resonated with you the most? What will you try to do differently? Who can you engage with to support your journey?

Outstanding frontline managers don't happen overnight, and they certainly aren't born into capable leadership. Excellent managers become such by deliberately working on their effectiveness, and you're on that path. You have spent time with this book in order to consider your own leadership journey and have considered ways to avoid the common mistakes that new leaders make. Most likely, you've completed some of the assessments and exercises outlined in the previous chapters. Now, set *your* intention.

I attended an outstanding coaching program a few years ago. Learning Journeys[5] helped me regain the valuable ability of asking great questions in coaching and reminded me to begin where the individual is on their own journey, not where you wish they were. The program encouraged us to set an intention. An intention is present-focused, as opposed to looking into the future. It is claiming what you will do, rather than identifying your desires and aspirations, and it is deep and intrinsic, rather than surface-level thinking.

What do you want? From your role, your life, yourself, and your team?	
When you get what you want, what will you have? Be specific; add color and nuance.	
What difference will it make? To yourself, to others in your life, and to your team?	

Now, write down your intention. Hang it in your office and put it on your phone. Refer to it often and share with a few people to help hold yourself accountable to becoming the leader you aspire to be. *Claim who you are as a leader.* What difference will it make?[6]

Final Thoughts

Just reading this book won't automatically make you a fabulous leader. It does, however, mean that you are interested in and committed to working at developing your highest leadership potential. As we said in the first chapter, you will make mistakes and won't get everything right—so lead with grace. Extend it first to yourself and then to your team. Be kind to yourself through the transition, and grant acceptance to yourself for when things don't go as planned. Remember, the tiltrotor Osprey was in development for over thirty years before it was operationalized in the marine corps.

Much of leadership is about effectively interacting with others. This final chapter, however, is about you. It includes a number of tips and strategies for maintaining yourself while supporting and maintaining your team. Effective leaders *must* take time to recharge, reflect, and regroup to truly be at their best.

Now *own your leadership voice.* Become the leader you aspire to become. Good luck and enjoy the journey!

References

1. Introduction to Carl Jung. https://en.wikipedia.org/wiki/Carl_Jung

2. Introduce to Archetypes. https://en.wikipedia.org/wiki/Jungian_archetypes

3. Overview of Discovery Insights. https://www.insights.com

4. Allen Church's work on manager self-awareness. https://www.researchgate.net/publication/14109411_Managerial_self-awareness_in_high-performning_individuals

5. https://www.learningjourneys.net

6. This analysis used by permission from: Learning Journeys International Center of Coaching, 2013. https://www.Learningjourneys.net

ABOUT THE AUTHOR

Janet Polach, Ph.D., is a global coach and leadership development professional. She has coached leaders around the world, including China, South Korea, Singapore, Puerto Rico, Switzerland, Ireland, the Netherlands, and the U.S. She believes all leaders can be great if they invest the time and energy into gathering feedback on themselves and focusing on their development. Janet's foundation for leadership started in the United States Marine Corps, where she achieved the rank of Lieutenant Colonel before retiring from the Marine Corps Reserves. She possesses deep academic knowledge in adult learning, leadership development, and coaching. Janet holds her Ph.D. in organizational leadership and development from the University of Minnesota.

Janet Polach, Ph.D.

I can be reached at *janet@inthelead.co*
www.inthelead.co
612.500.7069